Adventures Around
The Great Sacandaga Lake

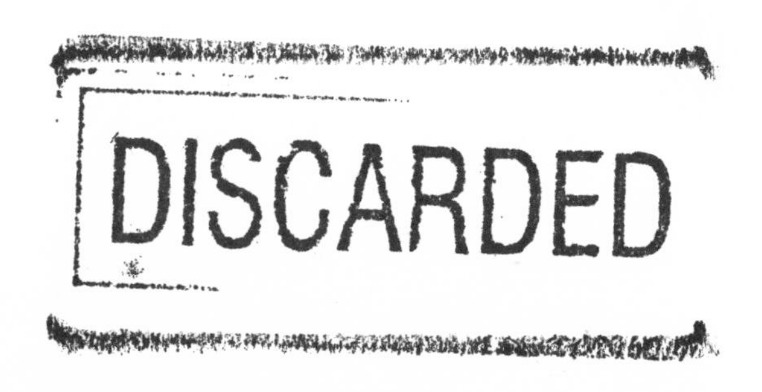

Adventures Around The Great Sacandaga Lake

Russell Dunn

Nicholas K. Burns Publishing
Utica, New York

Nicholas K. Burns Publishing
130 Proctor Boulevard
Utica, New York 13501

First Edition

ISBN 0-9713069-5-8

Library of Congress Control Number: 2002109516

Cover photo ©2002 Carl Heilman II
Photo taken from an outlook in the Town of
Day, N.Y. — July 2002

To my wife, Barbara,
whose constant companionship and support
made these adventures possible.

CONTENTS

Preface

It was destiny that I would fall under the spell of the Great Sacandaga Lake. Not only was I fascinated by the boundless opportunity it provided for adventure on land, sea, and in the air, but also by the lake's history.

But it wasn't always the case that I was so passionate about the Great Sacandaga Lake.

In my essay *Hats Off to Hadley*, for instance, I write that my first glimpse of the lake from the summit of Hadley Mountain in the early '80s led to no thoughts deeper than a token recognition that I had seen a body of water off in the distance. In 1986, in the essay *20,000 Leagues Under the Sac*, I tell how Barbara and I completed our open water scuba dive for PADI (Professional Association of Diving Instructors) certification, but the truth is that neither of us paid much attention to the lake. I just remember it being a punishingly cold body of water. In both instances, the lake simply served as background to the activity at hand. It's unlikely that either Barbara or I realized that what we were looking at wasn't just a lake, but an enormous reservoir of such size and dimension that it dwarfed all other nearby bodies of water, except for Lake George.

All of this changed in 1988, however, when an elderly woman named Mary Matney offered to give me a tiny eight-by-twenty-foot trailer located right on the edge of the Great Sacandaga Lake in the Sacandaga Trailer Park (now Adirondack Foothills RV Campgound). The trailer had proven to be too much for Mary to maintain and pay for in her later years, and had become a liability by the time I met her.

Barbara and I drove up to the lake for a quick look, not certain if we really wanted to take on this level of responsibility. At that time, you see, we were just dating, and didn't have any future plans to be together.

When we finally located the trailer, which was located in a vast field of trailer camps, we were stunned by its appearance. It was in much worse shape than we had ever imagined. Contact paper was peeling off in strips from the ceiling; water damage was rampant, as though the trailer had been dipped into the lake like a doughnut and pulled out to drip dry; there was no toilet, just a hole in the bathroom floor; and there was no running water, shower, or stove. To put it succinctly, the trailer lacked any of the basic amenities you would expect, even from a camp.

Despite the obvious deficiencies, we decided to take the trailer off of Mary's hands, envisioning that it would at least provide us with a tiny shelter where we could change our clothes in between adventures and a refuge if the weather turned downright nasty. We were operating under no illusions. The owner of the park had made it perfectly clear that we would have to haul the trailer away if we weren't able to bring it up to his standards.

Initially, we had assumed that the trailer would simply be an incidental part of our lives—a tiny foothold on the GSL, with no other significant meaning.

What happened, however, was something that neither of us expected. As we toiled to clean up the trailer, waterproof its roof, install a toilet, and reconnect running water, Barbara and I slowly grew closer and closer together as a couple, and the trailer became our special place—our Shangri-La—separate from Barbara's house in Albany, and my house in Scotia. Were it not for the trailer and the nesting experience it provided us, Barbara and I may never have gotten married, eventually ending up with a small lake house near Diamond Point.

It's fair to say, then, that my passion for the Great Sacandaga Lake is forever intertwined with the passion that developed simultaneously for Barbara as we explored the lake area and built our life together.

In terms of how this book came to be written, it started humbly, with me writing a few humorous articles for the *Sacandaga Times*, and then expanding the material submitted to include historical and geological facts about the lake. Later, the idea began to grow in my mind to put the articles into a book where, unlike pieces in a newspaper that fade into obscurity, the articles would endure for (hopefully) centuries to come.

The book was also a reflection of my professional life as a medical social worker for the Visiting Nurse Service Association of Schenectady, Inc., a home health care agency where I worked. For years, I had been writing up psychosocial assessments of clients and families.

All at once, I realized that I was now doing the same, only on a much grander scale—writing up a psychohistory of how the Great Sacandaga Lake came to be, and of how all the parts came to fit together to make a whole.

I am pleased with the way my life has turned out over the last decade or two. And were it not for one act of kindness on the part of an elderly woman, I might never have married Barbara, gotten to live up at the Great Sacandaga Lake, or written this book!

I acknowledge with special thanks Mary Matney, whose kind generosity provided us with an introduction to the Great Sacandaga Lake; Joe Zoske and Richard Delaney for their significant editorial comments; and the many wonderful people at the Great Sacandaga Lake. They truly are the people who have made the Sacandaga Lake *Great*.

Permission to use the following material is also gratefully acknowledged:

"The Great Sacandaga Lake: Older Than You Think," *Adirondac* (the magazine of the Adirondack Mountain Club, Inc.) (September/October 1994).

"Buoys of Summer," *Adirondack Life Annual Guide* Volume XXVI, no 4, (1995) page 82.

"Sailing on the Great Sacandaga Lake," *Sacandaga Times* (February 1993).

"Becoming a Ya-ho-er Has Its Drawbacks," *Sacandaga Times* (March 1993).

"The Continuing Adventures of Barb & Russell," *Sacandaga Times* (April 1993).

"Travels with Barb & Russell," *Sacandaga Times* (May 1993).

"Continuing Adventures of Barb & Russell," *Sacandaga Times* (June 1993).

"In Search of Kunjamuk Cave," *Sacandaga Times* (August 1993).

"Unexpected Inspiration Finds Italian Gardens of Broadalbin," *Sacandaga Times* (June 1995).

"If Hiking Moose Mt. Take a Compass Along," *Sacandaga Times* (September 1995).

"Night of the 80 MPH Winds," *Sacandaga Times* (August 1995).

"20,000 Leagues Under the Sac," *Sacandaga Times* (July 1997).

"The Great Sacandaga Lake From a Parachute," *Sacandaga Times* (August 1997).

"Pre-Reservoir Days," *Sacandaga Times* (October 1997).

"What Would Happen if the Great Sacandaga Lake Flooded?" *Sacandaga Times* (June 1998).

"Going to Bat for Bats," *Sacandaga Times* (July 1998).

"Optical Illusion," *Sacandaga Times* (July 1998).

"Rockwell Falls," *Sacandaga Times* (August 1998).

"Tenant Creek Falls and the High Diving Dog," *Sacandaga Times* (August 1998).

"Noise on the Lake," *Sacandaga Times* (September 1998).

"A Clute View," *Sacandaga Times* (October 1998).

"Water, Water, Everywhere," *Sacandaga Times* (April 1999).

"Only the Dead Know," *Sacandaga Times* (June 1999).
"What's In a Name?" *Sacandaga Times* (July 1999).
"The Moving Finger...." *Sacandaga Times* (August 1999).
"Sand Island Magic," *Sacandaga Times* (September 1999).
"Bald Bluff," *Sacandaga Times* (October 1999).
"The Old Man and His Horse," *Sacandaga Times* (November 1999).
"The Ghosts of Griffin," *Sacandaga Times* (December 1999).

Introduction

Like many who come to visit or settle in the Sacandaga area, my wife, Barbara, and I have been impressed by the warmth and friendliness of the townspeople and valley residents, and by the tremendous history they carry with them of villages and communities permanently altered by a river valley transformed into a stupendous reservoir.

The Sacandaga Valley is not the first area where nature has been overridden by human technology, nor is it likely to be the last. Without a doubt, however, it represents one of the most ambitious engineering projects ever undertaken in the northeastern United States. After all, a lake some twenty-nine miles long, over five miles wide at its broadest, and covering forty-two square miles in parts of Fulton and Saratoga Counties (and a smidgeon of Hamilton County) appeared where only a serpentine river had existed before.

For this to have been accomplished—and the first proposal to flood the valley dates all the way back to 1867—hundreds of homeowners, farmers, and business owners had to relinquish their life's work and make way for the tree-cutters. Gangs of men swept through the valley from 1927 to 1929, cutting down all trees and bushes to a height of no more than twelve inches, and razing every building and man-made structure.

The achievement of this goal wrought tremendous social, emotional, psychological, and cultural changes upon not only the 1,100 inhabitants of the valley, who were forced to relocate to higher ground or move completely out of the area, but upon the surrounding residents as well, who now had to adjust to a completely transformed topography introduced by a lake containing 283 billion gallons of water, ten new bridges, and fifty miles of roadways that never existed before.

Over seven decades have elapsed since the dam was completed in March of 1930 and the valley turned into an immense lake. Within another decade or two, there will no longer be a person alive from these pre-reservoir days.

Barbara and I have been fortunate to meet and talk with residents who do remember the "good ol' days" and who, at various times, were able to provide us with firsthand historical and anecdotal stories about the area.

This book is a collection of articles and essays written over the last decade, many of which have appeared in the *Sacandaga Times, Adirondack Life,* and *Adirondac* magazine. Most of these articles are adventure-oriented or historical. Some try, and sometimes succeed, in being humorous, occasionally introducing bits of funny business between Barbara and myself as we seek out new adventures. Always, however, the main intent is to talk about a specific area of the Sacandaga Valley, and to interject interesting snatches of geology, history, and sociology.

To keep the book lively, I variously refer to the Great Sacandaga Lake as the "Sac," the "GSL," or the "Sacandaga Reservoir."

The chapters range from subjects as diverse as hiking up Potash Mountain, to editorializing about the growing level of noise pollution on the lake. Since none of the essays are very long, if a particular subject doesn't appeal to the reader, that essay can be skipped without any loss to the book's continuity. As an edited collection of many previously published articles, much duplicative material has been eliminated, but some still remains so that each article can stand alone.

Consider the following chapters a smorgasbord, then—a feast of Great Sacandaga Lake adventures—and snack accordingly.

HISTORIES and MYSTERIES

WHAT'S IN A NAME?

HOW THE VILLAGES AND CREEKS OF THE SACANDAGA VALLEY WERE NAMED

Drive around the Great Sacandaga Lake and you will pass through numerous towns, hamlets, and villages of varying sizes, many of which have peculiar sounding names. Just where did these unusual names come from?

To answer this question in as straightforward a manner as possible, let's take an imaginary journey around the lake, starting at its south end by Broadalbin, and ending up just west of Broadalbin at Vail Mills.

We begin in the village of Broadalbin, located in Fulton County—named in honor of Robert Fulton, a past governor of New York State. Although the name Broadalbin suggests, at first glance, a "broad expanse," perhaps of land, this notion is incorrect. According to Edward R. Gazda, in his book *Place Names in New York*, the name came from Breadalbane—a district in Scotland. Early records show that the name was first proposed by James McIntyre, an early settler. Before that, Broadalbin was called Fonda's Bush—with *bush* an old Dutch word for "woods"—perhaps because it was northwest of the village of Fonda, further down in the Mohawk Valley.

Proceeding northeast on County Route 110 from Broadalbin, we pass by several creeks with interesting and distinctive names noted by historic markers. At North Broadalbin, Frenchman Creek is crossed—a small stream which was named after an early French settler by the name of Joseph de Golyer.

Further up, just south of Fish House, is Hans Creek. The name came about following a boating incident involving Sir William Johnson—Johnstown's most famous historic citizen—and John Conyne. The two men were fishing one day in the Vly, at the mouth of "Hans Creek," when their boat unexpectedly lunged, tossing Conyne into the creek. Johnson had a good laugh about it, and from that time on called the stream "Hons" Creek, which is Dutch for *John*. At some point, the "o" was changed to an "a," and it has been Hans Creek ever since.

From North Broadalbin, we come to the tiny hamlet of Fish House. Most of Fish House no longer exists, having been inundated when the reservoir was created. The hamlet was officially known as Northampton until 1961, at which time it was changed to Fish House, taking its name from a fishing house that Sir William Johnson constructed near Vly (or Vlaie) Creek in the late 1700s.

Continuing further northward, we reach the hamlet of Batchellerville. Like Fish House, Batchellerville was once a thriving village, with over 500 residents, until it vanished when the valley flooded in 1930. The town was named after Sherman and Samuel Batcheller, two brothers who founded the community.

From Batchellerville, we continue northeast along the South Shore Road, which now becomes Route 7. The hamlets of Lakeview and Overlook are soon passed through. Both were named because of their great views of the valley and lake.

At the northeastern end of the Great Sacandaga Lake, one can cross over the Conklingville Dam, turn left, and begin driving southwest on Route 4, which is the North Shore Road.

Our first destination, on the way back, is the hamlet of Conklingville—only a short distance from the dam—named after its founder, Gurdon Conklin, who established a large tannery in 1848. For reasons unknown, by the turn of the century a "g" was added to the name, and the village became known as Conklingville. In its earliest days, the village was called East Day. Although quiet and barely noticeable now, the tiny hamlet went through a boomtown phase during the late 1920s when the dam was under construction.

Driving along, we pass through Day Center and then West Day—both named after Eliphaz Day, a prominent 18th century settler. Day came from Attleboro, Massachusetts in 1803, and before long was heavily involved in lumbering. Unfortunately, it was this activity that proved his undoing. Day drowned while driving logs down the Sacandaga River near Conklingville in 1827. The town, previously known as Concord, changed its name to Day in 1827 to honor Eliphaz Day after it was discovered that another town in New York State named Concord existed.

West Day was originally known as Huntsville in honor of the Hunt family who came to Day in 1871. Amos Hunt ran a tavern in the tiny hamlet.

Reaching Edinburg, we are back again near the main body of the lake. Edinburg, like Broadalbin, derives its name from the Old World, this time from the Scottish city of Edinburg. The town was originally called Northfield, but was forced to change names when another town by the same name was discovered. After the village was renamed Edinburg, it was initially spelled with an "h"—Edinburgh—but within ten years the "h" had disappeared, again seemingly for no particular reason.

The main stream in this area is Beecher Creek, which runs through Beecher Hollow where numerous mills and factories once existed. The creek was named after the Beecher family who arrived in 1802—specifically in honor of Eli Beecher, who built a sawmill and dam on the creek in 1828.

Turning northwest on Route 4, we now head up to Northville. Northville got its name due to its being the northernmost point in Fulton County. If you think this makes Northville the northernmost point on the lake, however, you are dead wrong. That honor falls to Conklingville, with Day Center a close second.

A quick drive through Northville takes us across the Northville Bridge, over the northwestern-most part of the Great Sacandaga Lake, to Route 30. Turning left, we proceed south on Route 30.

Our first destination is Sacandaga Park, of which only a tiny part survives from its heyday at the turn of the century. In bygone years Sacandaga Park was the "gem of the Adirondacks"—a wonderful resort area containing a dance hall, theater, sports island, roller coaster, golf course, three hotels, burrow rides, and more. The name, Sacandaga Park, came from the fact that it was on the *Sacandaga* River, and that it contained a huge amusement *park.*

South of Sacandaga Park, we pass through the village of Cranberry Creek. Very little of it survived the flooding of the Sacandaga Valley. The name comes from the wild cranberries that once grew along Cranberry Creek near Tamarack Swamp.

The next village on our way is Mayfield. Named after the 1770 Mayfield Land Patent granted to Francis Beard and thirteen associates, Mayfield today constitutes one of the main marinas for boats and sailboats. The village was settled around 1760.

Proceeding around the southwest end of the lake, we pass by remnants of Munsonville, a town which doesn't exist any more. The village was named after E. B. Munson.

Coming to Vail Mills, just west of Broadalbin, we reach the end of our circumnavigation. Vail Mills was named after William Vail, who built a gristmill and sawmill on nearby Kennyetto Creek—the former shortly after

1804. In earlier days, the area was known as Lower Bush, and also West (Fonda's) Bush.

Kennyetto Creek passes through Vail Mills, as it does through Broadalbin. The name Kennyetto is Mohawk for "snake trying to swallow its tail," which seems like an appropriate name if you look at a topo map and follow the contour of the stream as it twists and turns. The stream has also been known as The Little Sacandaga, principally because it is the second largest tributary to the valley.

Having reached Vail Mills, we have completed our trip around the Great Sacandaga Lake, whose name, "Sacandaga" (an old Indian name), means "flowing grass" rather than "flowing waters." But who could blame the Indians for not knowing that the valley would one day be dammed?

The lake, after it came into existence in 1930, was initially known as the Sacandaga Reservoir. Early attempts to name it Lake Sargent, after its grand designer and chief engineer Edward Sargent, or "Lake of the Laughing Waters," both met with failure, and probably just as well. Later, when it became apparent that the Great Sacandaga Lake was more than just a reservoir, with thousands of camps now built up along its perimeter, the obvious name became "Sacandaga Lake." Unfortunately, another lake by that same name already existed and, what's worse, was located at nearby Speculator. As a result, the word "Great" was added to distinguish the reservoir from the smaller body of water by Speculator—and the Great Sacandaga Lake it has been ever since!

ONLY THE DEAD KNOW

THE DEAD ARE DYING TO TELL THEIR STORIES

Occasionally, Barbara and I will stop at the Fish House/ Northampton Cemetery, and take a brief stroll along the rows of tombstones. It's not as morbid as it may at first sound. After all, if you really want to get a feel for the history of the valley, it helps to physically connect with a part of it, and cemeteries provide that unique kind of link with the past.

Located on Shews Hill, the Fish House Cemetery is not far from the St. John House, built in 1795 by Alex St. John. The cemetery affords a spectacular, nearly panoramic view of the Great Sacandaga Lake, lapping away less than fifty feet from the nearest tombstone. The old-time residents of the cemetery don't have to worry about the water washing away their graves, however. The graves nearest the water are the newest, with the older burial places located further up at the top of the hill.

Although idyllic in appearance now, the cemetery didn't always occupy a commanding view of the Great Sacandaga Lake. Up until 1930, Shews Hill and its cemetery overlooked the valley proper, at a spot roughly one quarter mile from the confluence of the Sacandaga River and Vly (Vlaie) Creek. Both stream beds now lie buried beneath the lake waters. It was at this confluence that the Sacandaga River, proceeding southeast from Northville through Osborne Bridge, suddenly made a wide U-turn, and veered northeast towards Batchellerville.

Vly Creek, in turn, made its way northeast from the area near Munsonville, carrying with it the waters from Kennyetto Creek, Beaver Creek, Frenchman Creek, Hans Creek, Cranberry Creek, Roberts Creek, Jacksons Creek, and Mayfield Creek.

The confluence of the Sacandaga River and Vly Creek, therefore, produced a great deal of converging water, and nearly every spring it was virtually guaranteed that flooding would occur in the low-lying portions of the valley, particularly around Fish House. In fact, it was because of the valley's relative flatness and proneness to flooding that engineers and legislators decided that the Sacandaga Valley would make a perfect reservoir site. In the early pre-reservoir days, it's important to bear in mind that Shews Hill overlooked a very different kind of valley: one filled with rivers and streams, marshy areas, forests, dense underbrush, and lots of game.

From the time that Fish House became settled in the late 1700s until the early 1920s, hundreds of people were buried on Shews Hill, with no one ever imagining how the cemetery might look in the future. To them, the Sacandaga was a valley, and always would be. Imagine their great surprise, then, if the dead buried in Fish House Cemetery could be brought back to life, even if only for a moment, for a glimpse of the area surrounding them. Instead of thickets of trees and an occasional passing canoe, they would see miles of unbroken waters, teeming with powerboats and scurrying jet skis.

The only consolation is that the dead in Fish House Cemetery, by good fortune, were buried on a hill that happened to be high enough to survive the valley's flooding. Others were not so lucky. According to Larry Hart, in *The Sacandaga Story*, over 3,872 people from twenty-two different cemeteries had to be transburied because they were interred in graveyards too low-lying to escape the watery reach of the reservoir.

Should you happen to be taking a stroll through the Fish House Cemetery, or any of the other graveyards surrounding the lake, it's worth looking at the tombstones and pausing for a moment to connect to the past through its dead.

IF THE SHEW FITS

THE SHEWS OF FISH HOUSE WERE MORE THAN JUST YOUR AVERAGE SACANDAGA VALLEY FAMILY

As you drive along Routes 110 and 7 on the southeast shore of the Great Sacandaga Lake through Fish House, you will see two historic markers, both with the name Godfrey Shew prominently displayed. Who was Godfrey Shew, and what was his relationship to the Sacandaga Valley before it became a reservoir?

A number of years ago Donald J. Sawyer wrote an intriguing book, entitled *They Came to Sacandaga*, which details Godfrey Shew's life from a young man to his exploits as an early settler in the valley. The story of Godfrey Shew is really a story about how the Sacandaga Valley became less a wilderness and more a civilization.

Shew was born in Germany in 1710, son of a German nobleman, and developed, early on, an abiding passion to journey to the New World, despite the fact that this would necessitate leaving behind his parents, siblings, friends—literally everything that was known and of value to him. At the tender age of nineteen, Shew made the journey across the Atlantic Ocean, arriving in New York City after a rather harrowing trip. By a twist of fate, according to Sawyer, Shew immediately made the acquaintance of William Johnson, a man who later would become the predominant peacekeeper in the Mohawk Valley, respected by both Europeans and native Indians alike. During the French and Indian War, he fought under Sir William Johnson and was wounded at Fort Ticonderoga.

Years later, when Johnson, then elevated to the status of "Sir" William Johnson, offered Shew one hundred acres of land in an area of wilderness north of the Mohawk Valley, Shew, along with his wife, the former Katie Frey, and their two boys once again chose to leave the comfortable and known life to head off to Johnson Hall in what is now called Johnstown. The land that Johnson intended for Shew was in a wilderness area that Johnson used for fishing and hunting—a place where he had constructed a primitive fishing lodge that later came to be known as *Fish House*.

Shew first settled in the area of Fish House in 1762. His original house was destroyed in 1778, during the Revolutionary War, by a raiding party composed of Tories and Indians. Worse yet, Shew, and three of his sons, John, Stephen, and Jacob, were captured and taken north to Canada. Fortunately, Shew's wife and his other children hid and escaped capture. Godfrey, Stephen, and Jacob were later traded for Tory Prisoners, and six months after that, John made good his escape.

The family, reunited at Fish House, proceeded to build a second home in 1784, and it is this home, referred to as the *Shew House*, which still stands. In fact, the house happens to be one of the few existing eighteenth-century homes in the town of Northampton.

Godfrey's son, Jacob, later went on to serve in the New York State legislature in the early 1800s, and was a vocal advocate for the famous double barreled Fish House Bridge that was finally constructed in 1818, and which survived over a century until giant waves smashed the bridge to bits as the Sacandaga Valley was flooded.

If you visit the Fish House (Northampton) Cemetery, located just north of the junction of Fish House Road and County Route 110, you will come across several tombstones with the family name *Shew* on them. The monuments are located on top of the hill, surrounded by a black, iron picket fence. As a point of interest, the cemetery itself is located on *Shew's Hill*—named for its high ground above the valley, and also because Godfrey once stationed his son Jacob on the hill to scan the river and valley below for any signs of hostile war parties.

Godfrey Shew and his family have the distinction of being the first permanent white settlers in the area; with the historical lineage of the Great Sacandaga Lake and, in turn, the Sacandaga Valley going directly back to them.

THE OLD MAN AND HIS HORSE

THERE WERE VARIOUS WAYS THAT PEOPLE MOVED OUT OF THE VALLEY

On March 27th of 1930, Edward H. Sargent, Chief Engineer of the Sacandaga Reservoir, closed three outlet valves, stopping the waters of the Sacandaga River from passing through Conklingville; and so was created the Sacandaga Reservoir—a project that many, earlier in the century, had thought too ambitious to ever reach completion.

Work began on the Great Sacandaga Lake in 1927 when gangs of men started constructing the huge earthen dam in Conklingville. Over 500 laborers were deployed, and they worked steadily to create an 1,100 foot earthen barrier of gravel and cement to intercept the Sacandaga River.

At the same time, crews of workers swept through the valley, cutting down all trees and bushes. For several years, the sky was constantly filled with smoke from trees and bushes being burned in huge piles as the cutters relentlessly made their way through the valley.

But what about the homes that were saved?

Not everybody, you see, decided to abandon their homesteads and move out of the valley. Some hardy souls chose to stay and save their homes by physically moving the houses out of the valley onto higher ground; high enough to be above the water line when the valley flooded. This was made possible by the fact that New York State had only taken possession of the land, not the houses.

One of the villages facing extinction was the hamlet of Fish House, a community that once flourished north of North Broadalbin. During the early 1800s, Fish House grew into a bustling industrial center, with a variety of sawmills, chain factories, harness shops, blacksmiths, tanneries, and associated businesses. By the beginning of the twentieth century, however, the town had become less industrialized, and had matured into an elegant village, with elm-lined streets and magnificently constructed classic homes. Its inhabitants were chiefly wealthy, conservative landowners.

In 1922, the Hudson River Black River Regulating District was established, and within several years, the villagers in Fish House knew that their town was doomed. Thus started a slow exodus from the valley, and so begins the story of the old man and his horse.

George Buell, an old timer who lived in the Fish House area for most of his life, clearly remembered how the houses were moved, for as a boy of sixteen years he watched a man from Ballston Spa and his bay horse single-handedly haul twelve of them out of the valley. The horse, according to George, was more intelligent then most men, and would follow the old man's every command. Together they worked as a team.

First, each house was jacked up and logs placed under the floor beams to act as rollers. The old man then dug a hole some distance uphill from the house, drove in a drum, and placed rocks around the barrel to hold it securely in place. The drum served as a fulcrum.

One or two long cables were next connected to the house so that the structure could be pulled as one unit. The old man subsequently harnessed his horse to a long rod that extended from the barrel. Following the old man's commands, the horse slowly walked in circles around the barrel, and the house was gradually leveraged uphill, foot by foot. So closely did the man and horse work together that if the old man told the horse to take three steps and then stop, it would! After the house had been dragged uphill for roughly one hundred feet, the old man would dig a new hole further up the hill, and repeat the process for as many times as it took in order for the house to be sufficiently moved high and dry out of the valley.

If you happen to drive through Fish House, you will notice that there are a number of homes on or near the main road, County Route 110, which were once located further downhill in the valley. One home is locally known as the "Brady Home," after a prior elderly owner. The three story house is located on Route 110 about two tenths of a mile south of the junction of Fish House Road and Route 110. If you're ever invited into the house, be sure to look at the old picture of the home which rests on the living room mantle. The photo shows the house as it once stood in the village of Fish House, right on the crossroad at the center of town where travelers would head one way to Sinclair Point and the other way towards the Vly.

The Marvin House, which was intentionally burned to the ground in June of 1996, also once served as an example of a house reclaimed from the valley floor. Originally, the house was located at the confluence of the Sacandaga River and Vly (Vlaie) Creek before it was brought up near to what is now the Silver Maple Park. There are a number of other homes in Fish House that were moved and still survive. There are even huge, curved beams from the famous Fish House Bridge that still exist. These beams were incorporated into a garage that was commercially run by Minnie Hoffman under the name *Cabin Crafts*.

Parts of *old* Fish House live on, and all because of one old man and his horse.

THE MARVIN HOUSE IS NO MORE

SADLY, ANOTHER PIECE OF SACANDAGA HISTORY GOES UP IN SMOKE

In June of 1996, we saw smoke billowing into the sky just north of Diamond Point. Being curious, and in need of a little extra exercise, the two of us threw our canoe into the lake waters by our camp, and paddled off in the direction of the smoke.

Fifteen minutes later, we had reached the shore, where fire hoses stretched from the lake across rocks to a long lawn, and from where we could see people milling around a house that was totally engulfed by flames. There were firefighters everywhere standing by, ready to spring into action in case the fire got out of hand and invaded the surrounding area.

Inadvertently, we had come upon the immolation of the historic Marvin House, adjacent to the Silver Maple Park. For Barbara and me, it was hardly an unknown area, for we had visited the house several times in the past, having walked down a shady lane from a historic roadside marker on County Route 110, just about a half mile south of the intersection of Fish House Road and County Route 110. During our last visit on foot, the Marvin House was still standing, but obviously in much need of maintenance and, from a structural standpoint, of questionable integrity. At the time, however, it never occurred to us that a historic landmark like the Marvin House would be torched and intentionally brought down, much as the famous Catskill Mountain House near Haines Falls was in 1963.

According to the historic marker, the Marvin House was built in 1815 on the site of Sir William Johnson's fish house. The builder of the home was David Marvin, a revolutionary war soldier from Connecticut, whose family continued to occupy the house after his death. David Marvin was buried in the Presbyterian Church graveyard, which is located in the hamlet of Fish House.

From 1815 to 1929, the home stood its ground. Then something unexpected and totally unplanned occurred—the construction of the Sacandaga Reservoir. With much effort and toil, the house was moved uphill and out of the valley to its location near County Route 110, so that it might be preserved. And here it sat for another sixty-six years until fire did what water was not able to accomplish; the complete and total destruction of the Marvin House.

While throngs of spectators, interspersed by firefighters, looked on and chatted quietly, Barbara and I watched solemnly. It was a sad feeling to see part of the Sacandaga Valley's history vanish in smoke. The following week we returned and, after strolling around in the flatness where a house once stood, left with a charred wooden piece of the house. It now rests on a shelf in our camp—a somber reminder of how history is vanishing so quickly around us.

Life goes on, however. A new house, much in the style of a modern-day European castle, has been built at the site of the old Marvin House.

THE MOVING FINGER WRITES...

ONCE THE DECISION WAS MADE TO FLOOD THE VALLEY THERE WAS NO TURNING BACK... ONLY LOOKING BACK

Very few of us can imagine how it must feel to put down deep roots in a community, to be forced to leave, and then to have that community become so unalterably changed that it becomes impossible to go back again.

While tornadoes and hurricanes may smash through an entire community, leaving behind only wreckage and downed trees, the general topography of the land still remains unchanged, and people are at liberty to return and rebuild their lives.

In the case of the Sacandaga Valley, this is not what happened. When the Sacandaga Reservoir was created, there was no turning back for those residents who were forced to abandon their homes and farms. In one fell swoop, the topography of the valley changed forever.

Still, there were doubters. Up until the mid-1920s, before definite plans were formulated and concrete actions undertaken to transform the valley, there were only a handful of valley folks who really thought that engineers would change the valley into a reservoir. After all, the Sacandaga Valley was hardly a barren tract of unwanted and undesirable land. It was heavily occupied, with towns and villages, bridges, farmlands, railroad tracks, miles of roads, trees, and even a renowned amusement park called Sacandaga Park.

Many simply scoffed at the notion that change would occur, believing, as most of us do, that tomorrow will pretty much be like today. To be sure, they had heard rumblings before about the valley being turned into a reservoir, but nothing had ever come from them. In 1895, for instance, the State Engineer and Surveyor, George W. Rafter, talked about building a twenty foot high dam at Conklingville to impound four billion cubic feet of water—and that was for merely 1/70 the volume of what was to become the Sac. No action was ever taken, however. To many in the valley, the task of creating an even larger twenty-nine mile long reservoir just seemed too fantastic a project to be undertaken.

Legitimate concerns and objections were raised, of course. What about the people who lived in the valley and who owned land; land that had been passed down from one generation to the next? Didn't they have a major say concerning the fate of the valley? And what about the dead? There were twenty-two cemeteries in the valley that would be affected. Who would speak for those who could no longer make their wishes known?

And, of course, economic objections abounded as well, as they always do. Sacandaga Park brought in a great deal of tourism to the area. What would the owners of the park say about the prospect of having their business shut down for good? And the Fonda, Johnstown & Gloversville Railroad—were their owners just going to roll over and play dead?

Obviously, history has proven that these objections were not enough to stop the valley from being flooded; for at the same time, there were also compelling reasons why a reservoir had to be created. Foremost was the need to control the flooding of the Hudson River by turning off the spigot of one of its largest tributaries—the Sacandaga River. The year 1902 had been a bad year for flooding; 1913 had produced three flash floods that had even precipitated an epidemic. Objectively speaking, even in a good year the Hudson River could be unpredictable, turning mean and ugly with hardly any notice and wreaking havoc on the public at large in the Hudson Valley.

There were also secondary reasons: the well publicized need to increase water flow in the Hudson River during dry spells, so that the Atlantic wouldn't push too far upstream and contaminate fresh water deposits downstate, and the need to create hydroelectric power at the Stewart Bridge Dam station.

With the needs of the thousands being outweighed by the needs of hundreds of thousands, the die was cast in favor of the reservoir, and the Hudson River Regulating District was created in 1922 to see to the reservoir's implementation. It is probably fair to say that it wasn't until 1927, however, that the valley folks were finally forced to come to terms with the fact that change was an inevitability. For it was in that year that the cutters began working their way through the valley, slashing down trees and literally scouring the earth.

They say that in the fall of 1929 many people deliberately drove through the valley, winding their way along the interconnecting roads, through villages that no longer existed, and past forests that no longer held trees, simply because they knew they could never do it again.

And so, the topography of the Sacandaga Valley changed forever in 1930 when the valley was flooded.

Still, there are glimpses of the past. Every once in a while during a particularly dry spring and summer, the waters of the Great Sacandaga Lake contract further than normal, and vast areas of the lake bottom are exposed. When this happens, it is still possible to glimpse an old road, the faint outline of a foundation, or an old stone boundary wall.

And every once in a while the thought passes through my mind about how strange it would be if the Conklingville Dam gave way, and the Sacandaga Valley once again became an area of swamps, streams, and farmlands. Wouldn't it be a weird feeling to live again in a house on the valley floor, knowing that once, decades before, there were waves breaking thirty feet above the top of your house?

HOW BIG IS "BIG?"

IT'S BIGGER THAN YOU THINK!

Objectively speaking, the Great Sacandaga Lake is of respectable size: twenty-nine miles long, over five miles across at its widest, with a shoreline perimeter of 125 miles. It covers 29,000 acres of land, or the equivalent of forty-five square miles, and contains 283 billion gallons, or what is equal to 37.8 billion cubic feet of water. But what do these dimensions mean in comparison to other sizeable bodies of fresh water?

If we want largeness, we don't have to look very far. The United States contains the largest grouping of fresh water lakes in the world—the so named *Great Lakes* (Superior, Michigan, Huron, Erie, and Ontario). How does the Great Sacandaga Lake compare with these Great Lakes? To make it as fair as possible, let's compare the GSL with Lake Ontario, the smallest of the Great Lakes, part of which also happens to comprise New York State's northern perimeter.

Even though Lake Ontario is less than one quarter the size of the largest Great Lake, Lake Superior, it simply dwarfs the Great Sacandaga Lake in terms of sheer magnitude. Lake Ontario encompasses 7,340 square miles, which gives it a surface area some 163 times greater than the Sac's. Or, to put it even more graphically, Lake Ontario is about the size of New Jersey. Clearly, no reservoir can compete with a lake the size of a state!

Even depth-wise, the GSL falls far short of Lake Ontario. Whereas the Great Sacandaga Lake's deepest point is just over seventy-five feet, which is where the bed of the original Sacandaga River can be found, Lake Ontario goes down to 802 feet! And if we look at Lake Superior, matters get even worse. Lake Superior is 1,333 feet at its deepest.

But even Lake Superior is by no means deep as far as deep lakes go. Lake Baikal in Siberia has a depth of 5,700 feet, more than a mile straight down, making it the deepest lake in the world, and some eighty-one times deeper than the Great Sacandaga Lake.

Perhaps, when all is told, it is not fair to compare the Great Sacandaga Lake to the world's largest or deepest lakes. Let's turn, then, to the second largest body of water in New York State, Lake Champlain, named after the Frenchman Samuel de Champlain, who "discovered" it in 1609. Lake Champlain is a large lake, but by no means large enough to be considered one of the Great Lakes, although advocates have attempted, as recently as 1998, to have it designated as one. Lake Champlain measures 490 square miles, which is almost eleven times the surface area of the Great Sacandaga Lake, and is 118 miles long, and ten miles across at its widest. This is large. Even depth does not provide any solace if you are comparing lakes. Near Split Rock, Lake Champlain is 399 feet deep—nearly six times the depth of the GSL.

But perhaps comparisons with Lake Champlain are also unfair since Champlain, like Ontario, is only partially enclosed by New York State, sharing its boundaries with Vermont. How does the Great Sacandaga Lake, then, compare to other lakes that are completely enclosed within the state boundaries?

Oneida Lake, northeast of Syracuse, is a respectable body of water. Although deeper, and therefore containing a much greater volume of water, it is only slightly larger than the GSL if you go by surface area.

Then there are the Finger Lakes. It is immediately evident that the Great Sacandaga Lake is larger than several of the smaller Finger Lakes, and that the two largest Finger Lakes, Cayuga and Seneca, are not larger than the GSL by much. Both Cayuga and Seneca Lakes are roughly forty miles long and two and one-half miles wide. Seneca Lake covers sixty-seven square miles, and Cayuga Lake has a surface area of sixty-six square miles.

However, if we want to find a lake almost equal in size to the GSL, we don't have to look far at all. Lake George, also located in the northeastern part of New York State, has repeatedly been described as the GSL's twin sister, and for good reason. Lake George is thirty-two miles long, and three miles across at its widest—almost the dimensions of the GSL. But here the similarities end.

Lake George is considerably deeper than the Great Sacandaga Lake, being, in fact, 187 feet deep in parts; because of this, the lake contains a considerably greater volume of water. Lake George also has a notable maritime history, with hulks of boats resting on its bottom, therefore making it a more interesting body of water for divers to explore. The Great Sacandaga Lake has none of this. Essentially it is an underwater desert, with only eroding traces of foundations and artifacts from the days before the valley was transformed into a reservoir.

Once again the GSL seems to be outclassed. Maybe, however, by comparing the GSL to other large lakes we are still not giving the lake its just due. Maybe instead of comparing the Great Sacandaga Lake to large natural lakes, we need to compare it to other reservoirs in the state. After all, the Great Sacandaga Lake isn't a natural lake; it was built only seven decades ago, whereas the natural lakes of New York State were created by the power of retreating glaciers some 10,000 years ago. How then does the Great Sacandaga Lake compare against reservoirs like itself?

The Schoharie Reservoir—completed in 1924 by impounding Schoharie Creek, just six years before the Great Sacandaga Lake was created—is located at Gilboa, and is six miles long and three fourths mile across at its widest. Encompassing 1,145 acres, it is clearly a puddle in comparison to the Great Sacandaga Lake.

The Alcove Reservoir—a main water supply for the city of Albany—covers 1,400 acres, and is just slightly larger than the Schoharie Reservoir.

Likewise, the Pepacton Reservoir in Margaretville, which impounds the East Branch of the Delaware River, and the Cannonsville Reservoir, which impounds the West Branch of the Delaware River near Stilesville, are both tiny reservoirs by comparison. The former is eighteen and one-half miles long, 120 feet at its deepest, and encompasses 5,700 acres. The Cannonsville Reservoir is fifteen miles in length, 150 feet at its deepest, and covers 4,800 acres.

Neither, however, occupies much more than one-sixth the surface area of the Great Sacandaga Lake.

The Ashokan Reservoir near Kingston, however, is a more respectable contender. Completed in 1919 by impounding the Esopus Creek, the reservoir covers 10,000 acres, one-third of the Great Sacandaga Lake's surface area, and contains 132 billion gallons of water, which works out to almost one-half of the Great Sacandaga Lake's holding capacity—the reason being that the Ashokan Reservoir's greater average depth of forty feet allows for a larger volume of water to be contained.

There is no reservoir, however, that comes even close to matching the Great Sacandaga Lake in size, either in terms of surface area or cubic gallon capacity.

So, there you have it. The Great Sacandaga Lake may be pint sized next to the Great Lakes, but it is a respectable body of water in comparison to most of the New York State lakes (even if it may fall short on occasion), and is clearly in a league of its own when compared to reservoirs like itself.

THE ARCHITECT OF THE RESERVOIR

A BRIEF BIOGRAPHY OF EDWARD HAYNES SARGENT

Many people who enjoy the Great Sacandaga Lake are surprised when they come to learn that before 1930 the lake was actually a river valley, filled with trees, farms, covered bridges, and whole communities of towns and peoples.

So monumental did the task appear—clearing away hundreds of square miles of trees and brush, building an 1,100 foot long, 115 foot high dam in Conklingville, moving twenty-two cemeteries to higher ground, and dealing with intransigent settlers who refused to forsake their homes—that many doubted whether the job in fact could ever be done.

As history is quick to reveal, the task indeed was accomplished, and was done with such precision that when the lake later filled with water, its shoreline exactly matched the perimeter formed by the trees that were left uncut.

Who, then, was the architect of the GSL—the man responsible for implementing a plan first proposed by Samuel McElroy in 1867 to control the flood waters of the great Hudson River? His name is Edward Haynes Sargent, and there are still a few locals who maintain that the lake should have been named *Sargent Lake* in his honor.

Edward Sargent was born on August 24, 1885 in Newburyport, Massachusetts—the son of a man who ran a heating and plumbing business, and a mother who, unfortunately, died when Sargent was only seven years old.

Quite likely, young Sargent's destiny became shaped by his dad's professional interests, and Sargent's natural inclination towards engineering.

In 1907, Sargent graduated from the Massachusetts Institute of Technology and, almost immediately, became forever intertwined with New York State when he took a position with the New York City Water Supply Department. During the same year, Sargent also became Assistant Engineer with the New York State Water Supply Commission.

1909 was probably the next most important date for Sargent, for this was the year that he married Emma Olmstead (a native of Northville), in a ceremony performed in Northville, and began a close and enduring personal relationship with the Sacandaga Valley.

After having his career interrupted by being called to serve in World War I, where he was a major in the American Expeditionary Forces, Sargent returned to civilian life and resumed his duties with the NYS Water Supply Department, which now had become the NYS Conservation Commission, and continued at this post until 1923.

It was in 1923 that Sargent's path and the Sacandaga Valley's crossed again. New York State needed a capable person to spearhead an ambitious project that involved damming up the Sacandaga River and creating a huge reservoir. Sargent took the job and seven years later the Great Sacandaga was a fact accomplished.

Edward Haynes Sargent died in 1954, but a part of him still remains, in a manner of speaking, overseeing the lake that he was responsible for creating. At the Edinburg Cemetery, just one mile west of the intersection of Route 4 and Sinclair Road and virtually overlooking the reservoir, can be found Sargent's cemetery plot and tombstone. If you drive into the cemetery and proceed to roughly the northeast corner next to Wheeler Road, you should have no difficulty locating the tombstone. It is the only monument with a chiseled outline of the Great Sacandaga Lake on it, and an epitaph that says:

Edward Haynes Sargent
(1885-1954)
Major A. E. F. 116th Engineers
Designer and Chief Engineer. Sacandaga Reservoir

10,000 YEARS AGO

Before the Sacandaga Reservoir, there was another lake

During the decades of preparation prior to the lake's creation, thousands of trees were cut down, graveyards exhumed, barns and bridges razed, and towns relocated to higher ground. So thoroughly was this job done, and so completely have summer camps and year-round homes cropped up around the reservoir like a second-generation forest, that the casual visitor can easily be forgiven for thinking that the Great Sacandaga Lake has existed in its present state for time immemorial.

It may come as a surprise, then, to learn that the lake actually existed once before, many millennia ago, and that the shoreline of the present Sacandaga Reservoir virtually matches the shoreline of this ancestral, naturally formed lake.

To understand better the geological forces that brought all this about, we must travel back in time, tens of thousands of years ago prior to the last Ice Age, when the proto-Sacandaga River, ancestor of the present Sacandaga River, was a main conduit for the southern Adirondacks. The one striking difference between this ancient river and the present Sacandaga River is that instead of reversing direction below Northville and then traveling east to the Hudson River—the path currently followed by the Sacandaga— the proto-Sacandaga River, according to some geologists, headed unswervingly south, emptying directly into the Iro-Mohawk River, ancestor to the present Mohawk River.

During the last Ice Age, which is called the Wisconsin Glaciation, most of New York State was buried under thousands of feet of glacial ice, including all present lakes and rivers. When this final period of glaciation came to an end some 10,000 years ago, the retreating glacier left behind massive deposits of sediment, creating a gravel-rich barrier between Broadalbin and Gloversville that blocked the proto-Sacandaga River from retracing its pathway through the Sacandaga Valley down to the Mohawk River. The action of glaciers also had a similar effect to the northeast of the Sacandaga Valley, where huge moraines caused Lake George to form.

As can be readily discerned by driving around the Great Sacandaga Lake, the Sacandaga Valley is defined rather markedly by two prominent foothills, one on the eastern side of the lake, and one on the western. With these foothills forming natural sidewalls, it was inevitable that the valley would fill with water when the southern tier near Broadalbin became blocked by glacial residue. The result was that a Y-shaped lake formed, virtually indistinguishable from the present Sacandaga Reservoir.

Since this post-glacial lake was river-fed, the waters had to exit somewhere, and this proved to be at its lowest point of containment, in Conklingville. After leaving Conklingville, the turbulent waters eventually found the path of least resistance, which brought them into the Hudson River at Hadley.

As centuries turned into millennia, the erosive power of the Sacandaga River deepened its riverbed through Conklingville. At the same time, the water level of the lake began to drop as the height of the lake's containing wall was worn down where the waters exited. Finally, when the height of the spillway became no greater than the lake bed itself, all remaining waters disappeared, leaving the Sacandaga Valley dry again with the exception of the Sacandaga River, now following its irregular course around Sinclair Point, and northeast through Conklingville.

Within a short time, forests reclaimed the valley, and the marshy areas that were left, most notably The Vly, filled with lush vegetation and small animals and birds. Despite the rapid return of plants and animals into the valley and their tendency, along with wind and water, to obscure geological features quickly, the aftereffects of glaciation on the Great Sacandaga Lake are still very noticeable.

For instance, the soil in the Sacandaga Valley is not only sandy but loaded with boulders, stones, and pebbles, all transported to their present location through the action of glaciers. Lakefront residents understand this only too well, constantly having to rid their beaches of rocks and boulders, only to watch as a new crop slowly rises to the surface—a phenomenon undoubtedly intensified by the seasonal expansion and contraction of the reservoir itself, which causes the shoreline to move up and down the beach front like a giant rake.

The sand and gravel deposited through glacial retreat did not uniformly cover the valley floor, however. Instead, the sediment and debris tended to cluster and congregate, forming hillocks and drumlins. Today, the peaks of these mounds rise above the lake's surface and form its various islands. Some, such as Sand Island, are virtually devoid of rock, while others, such as Rock Island—a shoal that typically emerges in late summer when the lake elevation drops—have high concentrations of rock.

Those who have explored the lake using scuba gear report that its bottom is relatively featureless; just miles and miles of sand and mud. Apparently, there is little that remains from the pre-reservoir days to be seen by curious eyes. Furthermore, because the Great Sacandaga Lake is artificially created and of relatively recent origin, it has no maritime history and possesses no sunken shipwrecks to be explored. In this respect, the Great Sacandaga Lake has a history vastly different from its eastern cousin, Lake George.

If the original proto-Sacandaga River had not become occluded by glacial debris, but rather had continued down to the Mohawk River, it is interesting to conjecture what the Sacandaga Valley and affected areas would look like today. Let's start with areas outside of the Sacandaga Valley. To begin, we can assume that the Hudson River, from Hadley to Cohoes, would have been considerably less energetic and destructive than it is today. Obviously, the Sacandaga River's enormous discharge of water would have entered the Hudson further downstream, bypassing the numerous factory towns along its bank, such as Mechanicville and Waterford, which have been historically subjected to seasonal flooding. There would have been no outcry, at least from these towns, for the creation of a dam-controlled reservoir in the Sacandaga Valley.

Cities further south, such as Cohoes, Troy, and Albany, would not have seen any noticeable difference in the ferocity of the Hudson River. Joined by the Mohawk River at Peebles Island, with the Mohawk now carrying the waters of the Sacandaga River as well, the Hudson would have swollen to full size as it raced towards Troy and Albany.

However, one city to the west, Schenectady, would have had an appreciably different history. The Mohawk River, which currently passes to the northwest of Schenectady, is powerful enough to flood low-lying areas along the Mohawk Valley, as well as sections of Schenectady's historic stockade district, single-handedly. If the Sacandaga River had not been diverted by glacial debris, but rather merged with the Mohawk River west of Schenectady, the combined power of these two rivers would have made vast areas of current Schenectady literally uninhabitable during periods of seasonal flooding.

East from Schenectady, the Mohawk/Sacandaga River would have markedly affected the geology of the Rexford Gorge, Cohoes Falls, and Peebles Island, as it encountered each one respectively. Rexford Gorge, which is located east of Rexford Bridge in the town of Rexford, is a huge gorge with towering 130 foot-high cliffs on its northern flank. Faced with a more energetic and voluminous river to contend with, the gorge would have been cut deeper and wider. Cohoes Falls, approximately 2,000 feet upstream from the Mohawk's confluence with the Hudson River, would have been moved still further up the river, its sixty-five foot high walls of snake hill shale worn away all the more quickly by the Mohawk/Sacandaga's turbulent waters; and Peebles Island, exposed to a less powerful Hudson River and a more dynamic Mohawk/Sacandaga River entering from the west, would have been shaped and modified differently from its present configuration.

As far as the Sacandaga Valley is concerned, little change would have been noticeable, except for the direction of the Sacandaga River as it flowed past Sinclait Point and continued southward across the broad expanse of the valley. To be sure, the inevitable migration of loggers and trappers and related industries into the region would have ensured the development of towns and villages along the bank of the Sacandaga River; however, these towns and villages would have sprung up between Northville and Broadalbin instead of between Batchellerville and Conklingville, where they are currently found.

Predictably, the same clamor would have arisen to create a reservoir in the Sacandaga Valley so that Albany, Troy, and Cohoes could be spared the ravages of seasonal flooding. Only this time, Schenectady would have joined in the outcry, and probably with the loudest voice of all!

If politicians and engineers had built a reservoir, the dam would have been constructed between Broadalbin and Mayfield, not at Conklingville where it is currently found. For all practical purposes, the lake would be identical to the present Great Sacandaga Lake, with two minor exceptions: the location of the dam and the direction of the old riverbed under the lake.

Undoubtedly, a number of whitewater rafting companies would have formed and set up their base of operation below the dam. This would have been in the area of Broadalbin and Mayfield, however, and not in Haldey and Luzerne, where the companies currently operate.

But the best attraction of them all, coming down from the Sacandaga highlands into the Mohawk Valley, would have been the Sacandaga River itself, truly an impressive sight to behold. Perhaps its powerful waters would have forged an awesome ravine as it neared the Mohawk River, and a stupendous waterfall would have overlooked the valley.

No matter the course of history, though, it's reassuring to know that the Great Sacandaga Lake was probably destined to be with us as it is today—a lake for all time.

PRE-RESERVOIR DAYS

TAKE A TRIP BACK IN TIME TO SEE WHAT THE FLOOR OF THE VALLEY LOOKED LIKE BEFORE IT WAS FLOODED

For anyone who loves the Great Sacandaga Lake and its history, Larry Hart's book *The Sacandaga Story: A Valley for Yesteryear* is a must read. The book talks about how drastically life changed in the Sacandaga Valley when it was flooded. Unfortunately, reading passages about the old towns, roads, and bridges that once existed, and then trying to conceptualize how they relate to the present topography of the lake, can prove to be difficult indeed.

For this reason, then, you can imagine my absolute delight when I came across a 1939 reprint of a 1902 topo map of Broadalbin and the Sacandaga Valley area, with the current Great Sacandaga Lake superimposed on the old roads and towns that once crisscrossed the valley floor.

Suddenly, I was able to see with perfect clarity how all parts of the valley once related to one another.

Fish House Road, for instance, didn't just come to an end at County Route 110 in the hamlet of Fish House as it currently does; it continued straight across the valley and connected with Sinclair Road at Sinclair Point, and from there proceeded up to Edinburg.

And the two lane covered bridge featured on the cover of Larry Hart's book was part of this interlocking highway. The bridge was located approximately one-third of the way between Fish House and Sinclair Point, crossing what at that time was the Sacandaga River. Although the bridge was destroyed when the valley was flooded, parts of the main structure nevertheless survived, and became incorporated into several buildings in present day Fish House.

To the west of Sinclair Point stood the now defunct village of Osborne Bridge. Like Fish House, Osborne Bridge also had a covered bridge that crossed the Sacandaga River, this one being directly west of the present intersection of White Birch Road and Rulison Road as you look across the lake towards the Northampton Beach State Campground. In the early days, this road took you over or near to what is now Mead Island, and then onto the village of Cranberry Creek, which was completely destroyed except for six houses that were relocated to higher ground.

The third covered bridge to be found in the Sacandaga Valley was located at Batchellerville, but not where the present Batchellerville Bridge crosses over the lake. The old covered bridge, constructed in 1844, crossed over the Sacandaga River at some distance northwest of where Fox Hill Road intersects South Shore Road (Route 7). Folks in Batchellerville were then able to make their way into Edinburg, coming in at what is now known as Beecher Cove by the Edinburg Marina on the North Shore Road (Route 4).

Sand Island, a now popular destination on the lake for beach lovers and party-goers, was once a hill on the floor of the valley. It survived as the lake filled with water because of its higher elevation. At one time, a number of roads passed by the island. One highway angled out southwest from Fish House and then slowly turned south by Sand Island, ultimately connecting to North Broadalbin by Frenchman Creek. Another highway came up from Munsonville between Scout Island and Vandenburgh Point, and proceeded northeast until it intersected the Fish House/North Broadalbin Road.

During unusually dry summers, when the Great Sacandaga Lake is exceptionally low, vast underwater areas of Sand Island become exposed, and the rocky outline of an old foundation can be seen on the southeastern side of the island. Such "uncoverings" happen in other parts of the lake as well when the water level drops low enough, exposing bits and pieces of what once existed in the valley.

Before the reservoir was created, a wonderful lowland area of swampy marshes— beloved by sportsmen and known as The Vly—existed to the north, south, and west of Sand Island. Here, fishermen could fish for trout, bass, and giant muskellunge, and hunters could pursue rabbits, deer, muskrats, and migratory birds such as geese and ducks. The Vly was fed by a number of creeks, including Kennyetto Creek, Vly Creek, Beaver Creek, Frenchman Creek, Hans Creek, Mayfield Creek, Roberts Creek, Jackson Creek, and Cranberry Creek. All of this now constitutes the main part of the Great Sacandaga Lake.

In Larry Hart's book, a dramatic photo can be found showing railroad employees retreating along an unfinished railroad bed in advance of the rising lake waters. For whatever reason, the Fonda, Johnstown, & Gloversville Railroad had been given insufficient time to remove the tracks from the floor of the valley before the great flooding, and so were ultimately awarded $1,750,000 in damages. Ironically, they never used the moneys to reestablish a north line.

On the reprinted 1939 topo map, the ghostly outline of this railroad track remains, rounding the bend where the Grandview Marina is currently located, and continuing northward between the present mainland and Beacon Island until reaching the old underwater community of Cranberry Creek. From this point, the tracks continue northward, essentially along Route 30 between Tamarack Swamp and the Great Sacandaga Lake, reaching Northville at a point near where Route 30 and the present Northville Bridge intersect. The old train depot can still be seen in Sacandaga Park.

Sacandaga Park, once considered to be the "Coney Island of the Adirondacks," was for all practical purposes obliterated when the lake came into existence, with only vestiges of its past glory remaining. The outline of Sport Island, which was formed as the Sacandaga River divided temporarily into two branches just below Northville, rejoining a short distance later up above Osborne Bridge, remains forever visible on the old topo map.

Regrettably, this past will remain known on a firsthand basis to only a dwindling number of valley residents. For the rest of us, we must connect with it through libraries, documents, old topo maps, and some field work. Still, it is a journey fascinating and well worth taking.

THE BATCHELLERVILLE BRIDGE

THE PRESENT BRIDGE IS THE LATEST OF SEVERAL INCARNATIONS

Heraclitus, an ancient Greek philosopher, once said that "*there is nothing permanent except change*." This maxim is certainly apropos to the Sacandaga Valley in general, and to the Batchellerville Bridge in particular, for the present bridge is just one of several that have existed in the past.

The first bridge in the Batchellerville area was completed in 1802 and, since no lake existed at that time, its wooden planks spanned the Sacandaga River at a point about two miles above Fish House. This early bridge, according to records, was 200 feet long. Within twenty-five years, the bridge was destroyed, most likely by the torrential Sacandaga River which had a tendency to flood on a seasonal basis. A new bridge was constructed in 1817 and, rather astutely, was chained to the bank at each end so that it could literally float during high waters, thereby better accommodating the variable levels of the Sacandaga River.

In 1844 the bridge was replaced by a newer one, this time a covered bridge some 200 feet long. This new bridge led travelers into Edinburg through an area called Beechers Hollow, where the present Edinburg Marina is located. When the Great Sacandaga Lake was created, the old bridge was destroyed, and the present bridge was constructed—3,150 feet in length, with twenty-one spans resting on a series of concrete piles each over fifty to sixty feet high. Its load carrying capacity is fifteen tons.

But nothing forever escapes the wear and tear of wind, water, and time itself. The Batchellerville Bridge began to deteriorate so badly that in 1982 it had to be closed while the deck and railings were replaced. All during that summer and fall, two ferries transported passengers and cars between Batchellerville and Edinburg.

Currently, there is considerable talk that the Batchellerville Bridge will need to be replaced in the near future, since the 1982 repairs only provided temporary respite. A series of informational meetings have been convened by the New York State Department of Transportation to address a number of issues, including whether the new bridge should have a vertical clearance of fifty feet, instead of its present fifteen feet, to allow tall boats to access the full length of the lake.

Can the valley do without a replacement bridge at Batchellerville? The answer is resoundingly "no." The Batchellerville Bridge happens to occupy an extraordinarily strategic position by virtue of its location, allowing traffic to bypass the lake's two ends at Conklingville and Vails Mills by crossing in the middle. There is simply no other place suitable for a replacement bridge to be constructed.

That's not to say that people haven't considered other possibilities at one time or another. In the early reservoir days, builders had promised Fish House a bridge, and then later, a ferry service. Neither came to pass, and perhaps it's just as well, since a bridge crossing the GSL between Fish House and Sinclair Point—near where the lake is at its broadest—would have permanently and needlessly marred the natural beauty and elegance of the Sac.

To be sure, the Batchellerville Bridge and its successors are assured of a permanent place on the lake, with no other contenders in sight.

THE OLD RAILROAD STATION

HISTORY NEVER DIES; IT JUST GETS TRANSFORMED

In Kenneth B. Shaw's picture book, *Broadalbin Then and Now*, there are several interesting pictures of a railroad depot. My wife and I, curious to see whether the railroad depot still existed, drove into the village, brimming with confidence that we would find out one way or the other. Truth be told, we already had a fairly good notion of where to look, since the photos in Shaw's book suggested that the train station once stood where Bridge Street crosses Kennyetto Creek.

Much to our delight we discovered that the train depot is still standing and, in fact, is now occupied by an antique shop—a discovery that immensely appealed to our sensibilities. We walked around the building and found that the basic structure didn't look all that different than it had in 1913.

There are even old railroad tracks that have survived next to the station. They vanish as you walk west along Kennyetto Creek. In addition, an old building still exists adjacent to the depot. This building was evidently used by the railroad at one time.

In a leisurely manner, Barbara and I strolled down the dirt road behind the depot and followed it for a short distance until it ended at the Broadalbin Coal & Supply Company. From this point, a pathway continued on, leading through a short stretch of trees and bushes until coming out onto Fiber Lane by Fiber Conversion.

What we found interesting was that about halfway down this pathway you can see a section of the old railroad with tracks and beams resting on a series of trusses. The huge wooden beams are heavily charred, but whoever had tried to burn them down was only partially successful.

In another chapter of this book, mention is made that Miss Katherine (Kitty) Husted, a lady of high society, contributed generously to the village of Broadalbin. Miss Husted donated the town's first train depot, a picture of which can also be found in Mr. Shaw's book. It is said that Miss Husted drove in the last spike at an opening ceremony for the railroad line. Unfortunately, the building was destroyed by fire, and it is the second structure that now stands.

The Broadalbin Railroad began operating on October 31, 1895, transporting passengers between Broadalbin and the northern division of the Fonda, Johnstown & Gloversville Railroad (the FJ&G)—a distance of slightly over six miles. The FJ&G Railroad, in turn, provided Broadalbiners with access to Northville, Sacandaga Park, the twin cities Gloversville and Johnstown, Mountain Lake, and Fonda, as well as to the main railroad line going through the Mohawk Valley. The train service continued throughout the decades even as the automobile made trains increasingly obsolete, later transporting freight as well as passengers until 1956, when the Broadalbin line closed for good.

In 1958 the depot rather ingloriously became a laundromat. In 1971, a fire caused a fair amount of internal damage to the structure. Fortunately, the external damage was not extensive. At one point the village had designs to remodel the building and turn it into a town meeting hall.

The depot was ultimately purchased by Stuart and Erleen Hayes, who ran it as an antique store called The Depot for several decades. Then the building was purchased by Russell and Candace Hinkle, who refurbished it and are now operating it as Antiques At The Station.

By grace or good luck, the depot has survived the vicissitudes of both man and nature and still stands as testimony to the enduring tenacity of the Sacandaga Valley's past history.

THE GHOSTS OF GRIFFIN

VISIT A VILLAGE THAT NO LONGER EXISTS AND WHERE THE ONLY RESIDENTS NOW ARE GHOSTS

Between Wells and Speculator once stood a sizable village, the "boom town" of Griffin, complete with two hotels, a store, saloon, blacksmith's shop, tannery, sawmill, school, and over 250 homes. Settled in 1834, it was originally known as *Moon Mills*, then *Extract,* and finally *Griffin* in honor of Stephen Griffin, who operated a tannery in the village. Don't think about stopping in at Griffin for a quick nightcap and lodging, however, for the town vanished nearly a century ago!

Vanishing towns, to be sure, are nothing new to the Sacandaga Valley. When the GSL came into existence, it obliterated its fair share of small towns and communities, such as Fish House, Osborne Bridge, Batchellerville, Cranberry Creek, and Sacandaga Park, to name several. What makes Griffin different is that it vanished due to gradual and natural causes, and not as the result of a cataclysmic event, such as the valley being flooded and permanently turned into a lake.

Griffin was ultimately doomed because its existence depended principally upon the processing of lumber and hides and, like the mining towns that flourished out west while there was gold to be found, once those commodities started being used up in the local area, the town began to flounder. In 1893 the tannery shut down; then the sawmill. In 1895 the Girard Hotel closed its doors. After that, it wasn't long before the rest of the town dispersed, with townsfolk leaving in search of new dreams.

Griffin is now a ghost town—an example of what one hundred years of natural forces acting on abandoned and neglected buildings can accomplish. I say that it is a ghost town because you can walk right through the village and never even know it. Nothing remains except for old foundations and mortared blocks of stone, but these remnants are so fragmented and hidden that it would be easy to mistake them for rocky ledges or outcropping of rocks if you were hiking through quickly.

Griffin, however, is well worth the effort to find. Fortified with an old map of the town (which can be obtained from Barbara McMartin's book *Hides, Hemlocks, and Adirondack History*), it is still possible to traverse the terrain that Griffin once occupied and, with a liberal dose of imagination, reconstruct in your mind what the village once looked like.

Finding the site of Griffin is surprisingly easy, for the town rose up near the confluence of the Sacandaga River and its east branch. To get there, drive north from Wells on Route 30 for under four miles, until you come to the junction of Routes 30 and 8. Turn right onto Route 8, cross over the Sacandaga River, and continue northeast for roughly two and one-half miles.

On your right will be a pull-off for the trailhead to Cod Pond and Willis Lake. At this point, turn left onto a dirt road, and follow it downhill for two tenths of a mile. You will cross over an old iron bridge, built in 1903, that spans the East Branch of the Sacandaga River. As soon as you reach the other side, park off to the side of the dirt road.

As you gaze about from the stream to the woods and back again, bear in mind that you are now standing on the former main street of Griffin. One century ago, hundreds of homes and buildings stood along this section of the road, extending off into the woods. By walking due north, directly into the woods, you will readily come across a number of these old foundations.

There are no treasures to find—you can be sure that folks armed with metal detectors swept the area clean decades ago. There's just the satisfaction of reconnecting to a piece of the Sacandaga Valley's nineteenth century history.

Bring a lunch along, and follow a short path westward from the iron bridge along the north bank. It will lead you in a minute to Griffin Falls, which is small but pretty. From here, you can contemplate what life must have been like at the turn of the century; and, if you bring a copy of *The History of Hamilton County*, you can open up the book to the section on Griffin and, looking at actual pictures of the town, stare with amazement at how totally Griffin has vanished.

Truly, only the ghosts of Griffin remain....

JOHNNY IGOE

THE DEAD NEVER STAY DEAD FOR LONG AT THE GSL

Since water, by in large, is flat and featureless, what constitutes the face of the Great Sacandaga Lake is its towns, camps, marinas, and restaurants. Of these, it is the restaurants that prove to be the most captivating, for they are the places that we are drawn to in order to relax, celebrate, or just eat our fill.

I have in my possession an old issue of *BOSAC (*Volume I, No. 1), whose name stands for *Boating Sacandaga*. The pamphlet contains a roughly sketched map of the GSL, and the restaurants around its perimeter. Listed, in 1973, were: *The Barn* in North Broadalbin, operated by Emil and Adriana. Their slogan was, "It ain't the best, It ain't the worst. But it's the place to quench your thirst."; *Gate's*, north of North Broadalbin; the *Other Place*, run by Don and Dorothy Moss, and which featured dancing every Saturday night; *Sid's Place* near Benedict Bay, named after its owner Sid Dellaratta; The *Lonesome Lodge*, run by Ron and Alice Taggart; *Richter's Cocktail Bar* north of the Batchellerville Bridge; *Sportsman's Lounge* near Cranberry Creek; *Broken Spoke,* operated by Don and Bill Walrath; *Driftwood Park* at Vandenburg Point; *Muscle's Bar Harbor*; and *Twin Pines*.

Do any of these restaurants still exist?

If you take a quick drive around the perimeter of the lake, you will discover that all have either gone out of business, changed their names, or altered their identity substantially...

...All, that is, except one. That restaurant, also listed on the 1973 map, is the *I Go Inn*, located between Fish House and Batchellerville on County Route 7.

As it turns out, the *I Go Inn* also happens to be well known to us, since its location is only four miles north from our lake cottage. We have been going there since the late 1980s, and it has become a tradition for us to both start and end the season at the inn.

But who thought up the name?

Initially, we assumed that the name *I Go Inn* had been conceived as a play on words, with the meaning of the phrase dramatically altered depending upon whether you construe "inn" as a noun or a verb. Reinforcing this assumption was the fact that just several buildings north was the *Tumble Inn*—another establishment with a name that could be taken in one of two ways (and perhaps even in a third unintended way, for the building has been abandoned for some time and truly looks ready to "tumble in").

In light of all of this, then, imagine our total surprise when Barbara and I learned that the *I Go Inn* is not a contrived name, but actually based upon the name of a real live person who lived in the early days of the Sacandaga Reservoir—Johnny Igoe.

Igoe's legacy began when he built a small cottage in the Sacandaga Valley, putting it right where the *Inn* is currently located. The cottage, however, was never intended solely for recreational pursuits. Within a short span of time, Igoe had put picnic tables out on the front lawn and began briskly selling hot dogs to the tourists. As the business grew, Igoe enlarged the camp, adding on a wraparound L-shaped porch. Then, to increase the length of his season, he enclosed the porch, creating the basic structure that still stands today (minus a few recent modifications).

To enliven the atmosphere, Igoe would often play the piano and sing, encouraging folks to join in as the spirit (or spirits) moved them. This was during the days before juke boxes were in vogue.

A number of years later, Johnny Igoe sold his establishment to a businesswoman named Bernice, who ran the Maxwell House in Schenectady, as well as a dating service.

Bernice finally sold the inn to Hank Chelstowski, who was helping run the business for her. Under Chelstowski, the business prospered and became even more popular with the tourists.

In the early 1990s, due to illness, Chelstowski had to turn the business over to his son and daughter, Hank and Helen. And Hank and Helen have been running it ever since, with just one exception—1999. That was the year that the *I Go* failed to open its doors, staying closed throughout the season. To us, it looked like the days of the *I Go Inn* had finally ended and, with the *I Go*'s demise, the end of an era.

You can imagine our surprise, then, when we drove up County Route 7 in the spring of the year 2000 and saw that the *I Go* had reopened. We went in, ordered a pitcher of beer and some finger foods, and said hello to Hank, the affable proprietor. Not only was the inn back in business, but still under the same management.

Johnny Igoe and his dream had managed to survive into the Second Millennium after all!

IT'S ALL ON RECORD

THE LARGEST NORTHERN PIKE IN THE WORLD WAS CAUGHT AT THE GSL

In Sept of 1940—seven years after the Sacandaga Reservoir's creation—Peter DuBuc, a former Albany resident, was out fishing on the lake when he felt a tug on his line. A brief struggle then ensued, with DuBuc finally reeling in his catch—a northern pike that weighed in at 46 lbs. 3 ounces. Not only was DuBuc's catch the largest northern pike ever caught in New York State but, at that time, in the world as well.

To be sure, the odds are horribly stacked against a second record-breaking pike being pulled out of the Sac again. The area that DuBuc was fishing over happened to be The Vly—a huge marshland that existed prior to the lake's creation. Undoubtedly, it was the exceptionally well fertilized lake bed in this area that allowed for such an unusually large fish to flourish. Over the last sixty years, however, traces of the Vly have eroded away, leaving the bed of the GSL uniformly desolate.

HOLLYWOOD HAS SHINED ITS LIGHTS ON THE SACANDAGA VALLEY AT LEAST TWICE DURING THE LAST CENTURY

Around 1915, a movie called *Heart of Jennifer* was filmed near the former hamlets of Parkville and Osborne Bridge—two villages that later vanished when the valley was flooded. The movie starred Hazel Dawn, a well known actress of her day, and featured a number of local residents in the production.

In the mid 1990s, the movie *Billy Bathgate*, starring Dustin Hoffman, Bruce Willis, and Nicole Kidman, was released. The film included shots of Eggleston Falls and Fly Pond—two scenic areas above the northeastern shores of the Sac.

If this is the start of a pattern, we may have to wait patiently another eighty years for movie number three to come along.

AT LEAST ONE CELEBRITY HAS LIVED IN NORTHVILLE

Mel Graff, the creator of a nationally syndicated newspaper strip called "Agent X-9," resided in Northville during the 1940s. Supposedly, he used local names and roads in his strip in order to add realism and color to his stories.

SACANDAGA PARK—THE "CONEY ISLAND OF THE NORTH"—HAD AN UNUSUAL BEGINNING

Sacandaga Park was a famous resort area and amusement park just south of Northville. A little known fact is that the park began as a humble cluster of white tents pitched along the west bank of the river by a group of Methodists looking for a place to conduct religious services. The spot was so suitable and invigorating that the Methodists were soon joined by members from the Salvation Army and the Women's Christian Temperance Union. Out of this eventually emerged Sacandaga Park!

Northville is for the Birds

There are certain areas and towns in the world that seem to be natural destinations for birds. Capistrano has its swallows; Hinkley, Ohio its buzzards. Amazingly, Northville has its so called "chimney" swifts. For over three quarters of a century now, a flock of swifts that migrate over 7,000 miles from the Amazon jungle in South America has appeared in the skies above Northville. Like clockwork, in the early evening of May the 6th, they spiral down into an old, abandoned factory's chimney. There, in that same chimney, they build nests, and each year the cycle of life repeats itself. The chimney belongs to the former Hubbell Glove Factory and can be seen on the west side of Second Street.

THRILLS, CHILLS, and SPILLS

THE LAKE ALWAYS WINS

DON'T LET ANYBODY KID YOU. IF YOU GO UP AGAINST THE GREAT SACANDAGA LAKE, YOU ARE PLAYING RUSSIAN ROULETTE, FOR SOONER OR LATER YOU'RE GOING TO LOSE

Time and time again, we have seen trusting boaters, who moor their vessels off the east shore of the lake, underestimate the ferocity of the Sac. Many do so naively, believing that since they have taken every precaution and anticipated every possible contingency, their boat will be safe no matter how rough the lake gets. These are sailors who, obviously, have not heard of *Murphy's Law*. Neither are they aware that Murphy must have formulated his famous law while sailing on the Great Sacandaga Lake during heaving waves and an obliterated sky.

Five miles of open water can create winds of unbelievable intensity that hammer the shore line with four foot waves. Barbara and I know this only too well due to the fact that our camp is located squarely in front of just such a huge expanse of open water. While the wind is generally friendly—sweeping the air free of biting insects, and venting cottages when they becomes overheated—there are other times when all hell literally breaks loose (see *Night of the 80-MPH Winds*).

On more occasions than I care to remember, Barbara and I have had to run out of our cozy camp to help rescue a neighbor's boat—not ours, mind you, but someone else's. This is because the kind of sailing crafts we use—canoes, kayaks, and sunfishes—don't need to be moored out in the bay, waiting like sitting ducks for harpoon-like winds to take a shot at them.

One windy, stormy late afternoon, several years ago, we were relaxing, enjoying our happy hour of gin and tonics, when we heard a loud commotion coming from the beach. A neighbor's boat had just washed up and was being battered against the rocky shoreline. Mind you, this is a boat that we had to help rescue about two years earlier when its mooring line snapped. This time, the mooring lines had held, but the winds were so strong that the boat had been blown in to shore nevertheless, dragging anchor and all.

Have you ever seen a boat in the process of being reduced to kindling? It's not a pretty sight. Needless to say, with the help of a few drinks, a few neighbors, and a few feet of Sacandaga Lake water to flounder in, we were able to save the day—and the boat as well.

To be sure, Barbara and I have participated in and even mounted a number of boat rescues in our time, and let me tell you, maneuvering a large, heavy boat out of trouble can both challenge you physically, as well as turn out to be your worst daytime nightmare. Imagine wading into chest deep water and wrestling a thousand pound boat out of danger to a safe haven, all the while feeling like you're in the maw of an enormous washing machine.

Although a large boat may seem to possess considerably less weight when it is in water rather than resting on land, its mass remains unchanged, and mass is what counts if you suddenly find yourself between the boat and a large boulder. Make a wrong move and you can become a very unhappy camper if the boat rises up in the swell and comes down on you like a water buffalo.

Even if you go out and buy a rope that is as strong as Spiderman's webbing, and secure it to an anchor so heavy that even Popeye the Sailor couldn't lift it, there's still no guarantee that your boat will be safe when the GSL throws a storm at you. Allow me to illustrate my point. Several summers ago, a neighbor on our north side interrupted our quiet morning with a cry for help. He had noticed that a boat, belonging to one of the camp owners across the street, had suddenly acquired an unwanted companion. The two boats were now locked in an unearthly death grip, colliding viciously every thirty or forty seconds. The pattern was unvarying: one boat would slam into the second like a battering ram, recoil, retreat twenty or thirty feet, and then bounce back like a yo-yo on a short string.

The collisions were so loud that we could hear them from shore even over the full force of the shrieking wind and the pounding of the surf.

It was easy enough to reconstruct what must have happened. During the night, a boat from the opposite side of the lake had broken loose from its mooring, and was blown into our cove. By the worst luck imaginable, this rogue boat then became hopelessly entangled with the lines of our neighbor's boat—an eventuality that even the Olympian gods of the Great Sacandaga Lake could not have predicted in advance.

Unfortunately, despite the frightful abuse both boats were being subjected to, the tangled lines held firm, and neither boat would relinquish its hold on the other. We finally reached the neighbor who owned the moored boat, and he was able, after considerable effort, to disengage his battered vessel from the offending boat. Soon after, he hauled his boat out of the lake for repairs. By then, the police had already been contacted to see if they could find out who owned the rogue boat.

All of next day, the phantom boat remained moored off shore just as if it had always belonged there.

The following weekend, when we returned to the lake, the mystery boat was gone. I can only surmise that the police must have finally reached its rightful owner who came over and retrieved it.

Needless to say, it was a sobering experience for our neighbor who thought that nothing could possibly put his boat in harm's way.

Either way, as I said before, the lake always wins. It's not a question of *if*—just *when*!

Noise on the Lake

For better or for worse, the level of noise continues to grow louder with each passing year. Is there a limit to the decibels?

Although we are relative newcomers to the lake, the two of us have been visiting the area long enough to form some impressions of our own. One conclusion seems unshakably clear: the amount of hustle and bustle on the lake continues to increase with time, and in a way entirely different from past decades.

A recent look at an old postcard featuring one of the first motorboats on the Sacandaga Reservoir got me thinking about the so-called "good ol' days." It seems likely that seven decades ago the lake was not heavily used. Crisscrossing it were mostly sailboats, canoes, and rowboats, and only a smattering of engine-powered vessels. At that time, the lake was reasonably quiet and peaceful.

Over the last several decades, however, the number of motorboats has steadily grown to include speedboats and party barges, and to the point where they now outnumber sailboats. What has also increased, unfortunately, is the overall noise level of the lake, as though someone has slowly, decade by decade, been turning up the decibel level.

This increase in noise, to be fair, is not entirely the result of motorboats increasing in popularity and general usage. Since the Great Sacandaga Lake is over five miles wide at its broadest, and many more times as long, motorboats generally race along far from the shore, and create comparatively low levels of noise; perhaps a distant droning or rumbling at best. Although some motorboats, towing water-skiers behind them, still cling closer to the shoreline, they are in the minority, to be sure.

The noise level has gone up for other reasons, and perhaps these changes are irreversible. First of all, new technological advancements have increased the power of small cassette players and radios, producing thundering "boom boxes." Now, a single individual can literally flood an entire beach with ear-shattering sound, exposing people to precisely the kind of din that they left the cities to get away from. And, as a rule of thumb, I've found that it is precisely those people who thoughtlessly blast out their boom boxes who are least likely to turn down the volume when you ask them to do so.

But it is the advent of jet skis, or personal watercraft, more so than boom boxes that have forever changed the face of the Great Sacandaga Lake. Jet skis appeal to the young who like their excitement loud and fast. Almost without exception, the folks Barbara and I see jet skiing are teenage boys and young men, who use the vehicle not for transportation, but who parade the contraptions back and forth endlessly over a small patch of water, almost like young bucks vying for the attention and adulation of admiring females on the shore. You can probably tell from my tone that I am a little testy about jet skis. I am! Unlike motorboats, they remain close to shore, constantly racing back and forth, and creating noise pollution without precedent.

Jet skis, apparently, have little need for deep waters. What they seemingly do require is an audience, which generally is guaranteed by their proximity to the shore.

Today it seems as though the number of jet skis on the lake has increased to the point where almost every other lake user has one, just as color TVs gradually infiltrated the living room in the early '60s.

The first time I ever saw a jet ski was in the 1977 James Bond thriller *The Spy Who Loved Me*, and it was called a *wetbike* then. At that time, few if any jet skis were commercially available. How times have changed. Already I'm dreading what the next generation of jet skis will bring. Dare I even mention it for fear that my saying so will make it happen? Oh, the heck with it! My prediction is that the jet skis of the future will be equipped with booming cassette players and speakers that are waterproof and louder than ever. Then the noise pollution will be practically insufferable. I can only hope that the future is at least fifty years further ahead!

Addendum:

Noise On the Lake was written in the mid-'90s. Since then, New York State has passed new rules and regulations into law, specifically Senate Bill 5309-C and Assembly Bill 8097, which give towns, cities, and villages the power to regulate the presence and operation of jet skis on lakes within their jurisdiction.

I doubt, however, that these regulations will ever impact directly on the Sac, as the lake is quite simply too big and massive, and crosses too many municipalities.

Still, one can at least hope that jet skis will ultimately be required to stay a minimum of a half mile from shore. That, to me, would be an acceptable compromise.

OPTICAL ILLUSION

THERE'S A REASON WHY SOME FOLKS COULD NEVER ADJUST TO THE CHANGE OF THE SACANDAGA VALLEY INTO A HUGE LAKE

When I first stood on the rocky shore between Silver Bay and Diamond Point and looked out across the Great Sacandaga Lake, I would have sworn that the opposite side was only a couple of miles away.

"Someday we'll have to swim across," I remember telling Barbara with conviction.

Right! If we had tried it, chances are that we would both be in Davey Jones's locker now since neither Barbara nor I are, by anyone's definition, marathon swimmers. As we later learned, the Great Sacandaga Lake at its widest is five to six miles across—a distance that most swimmers would find intimidating.

To this day, I still marvel at how some objects can look so close, and yet be so far away. On the Great Sacandaga Lake, this is particularly true at night, when the flickering lights on the opposite shore only seem like a couple of city blocks away.

Mountains that are distant generally look bluish because of the intervening volume of atmosphere, and this becomes one way of estimating how far an object, such as a mountain, might be even though it looks close at hand. But what do you do if the atmosphere is unusually clear and the blue-ing effect is minimal, such as was the case when I first looked across the broadest part of the lake?

Some years ago Barbara and I attended an evening meeting of the Edinburg Historical Society, and listened to a speaker named Doug Parker give an impressive talk. What I found of particular interest was Doug's insistence that no books on the Great Sacandaga Lake have ever adequately recounted the anguish and mental suffering that the damming of the Sacandaga River imposed on its residents, many of whom had to move to higher ground, rebuild their lives, and cope with a topography that was totally alien from pre-reservoir days. According to one source, a couple of elderly farmers in Northville couldn't adjust to the change and committed suicide.

But what captivated me most of all was Doug's contention that there were a number of drownings following the lake's creation because the valley folks could not accept that their river had been turned into a lake; and not just any size lake, mind you, but one as large as Lake George!

Many locals would jump into their rickety old rowboats, never wearing or even bringing along a life-jacket (heck, who wore them back then anyhow), and would never be seen again. Presumably, they were guilty of underestimating the distance from one shore to the other, or of misjudging the ferocity of the Sacandaga as a lake. Like myself, perhaps these doomed folks also stood at the shoreline and said, before beginning their ill-fated trip, "It's only a quick jaunt over to the opposite side."

WHAT IF THE GREAT SACANDAGA LAKE FLOODED?

AN IMPOSSIBILITY, YES; BUT STILL, IT'S ALWAYS FUN TO SPECULATE

What would happen if the Great Sacandaga Lake kept increasing in height without abatement until the last island disappeared beneath the waves? How deep would the lake become, and what would be the consequences for low-lying lake-side areas?

Of course, we are talking about a virtual impossibility here. Even if it rained for forty days and forty nights, only so much water could be captured and contained in the reservoir before the Conklingville Dam, with water pouring over its spillway in a mighty waterfall, would release the excess volume. Since the Conklingville Dam spillway stands at 771 feet above sea level, it would seem that 771 feet is the maximum height to which the lake level could rise. At this height, no major changes would occur either in shoreline or island appearance.

Certainly in the past, the Great Sacandaga Lake has risen beyond its normal maximum operating height of 768 feet when unexpected rainfall in late spring adds to the reservoir's already significant height. When this happens, an additional three feet of emergency capacity allows the reservoir to fill up to the dam's spillway of 771 feet.

On rare occasions, when the unpredictability of nature conspires to raise the lake waters slightly above the maximum operating capacity, there has been damage caused to shorelines due to the powerful erosive action of the churning waters. Many homeowners have lake fronts with shorelines banked by massive rocks and boulders; even so, water can move huge rocks about in a willy-nilly fashion, and at times can even crest the top of rocky barriers, flooding lawns and eroding away grass and topsoil. Such is the life for homeowners who choose to live in camps and homes at the edge of a reservoir.

But suppose the waters of the GSL rose higher still than the maximum height of the Conklingville Dam. Suppose, for instance, that a huge earthquake struck, and massive slabs of rock and earth were dislodged from nearby hills and mountains, say from Woodcock Mountain near Conklingville, or where the Sacandaga passes between Gray Hill and Clute

Mountain, and that this debris settled into the narrow straits of the Sacandaga forming a natural barrier. Furthermore, let's say that the height of this new barrier was 805 feet above sea level. What would be the consequences of this natural disaster in which the waters of the Great Sacandaga Lake were dammed up even higher?

First of all, the water level of the lake would obviously begin rising, and appreciably so. After all, the Great Sacandaga Lake is fed not only by the Sacandaga River, which is substantial in itself, but by numerous smaller tributaries that, when taken as a whole, add up to a major contributory source.

The water level, however, would not rise at a predictable or predetermined rate. Rather, the time of year would be a major factor concerning the rate of lake growth. If the earthquake or damming occurred in July or during the later months of summer, the water level would rise slowly, since all tributaries would be carrying minimal loads of water. In mid-spring, however, the impact would be dramatic and awesome. Fed by winter's snow-melt, particularly from the southern Adirondacks, the reservoir would rise at a precipitous rate.

In either case, the lake would surely and ineluctably grow in size; the same result would be attained, just at a different rate.

What would become apparent to onlookers is that the Great Sacandaga Lake would increase in power and ferocity as it grew in size. With more water to act as muscle to rip at the shoreline and any obstacles standing in the way, the lake would be formidable indeed.

In Larry Hart's book, *The Sacandaga Story*, the sheer power of the Sac was demonstrated when the valley was initially flooded in 1930. Villagers in the hamlet of Fish House had hoped to save the Fish House covered bridge, but the surging waters of the Sacandaga reservoir literally ripped it to shreds before any rescue of the bridge could be effected.

We can safely assume that as the waters began rising, no buttress, piles of rocks, or fortifications fashioned by homeowners in an attempt to protect their properties would hold back the incoming waters. The GSL would become an irresistible force and the lake front a very movable object.

As the water level steadily rose, the effect on the islands would be noticeable. None of the half dozen or so islands stand that high above the reservoir to begin with, and most, generally, are fairly flat and broad, with no major high points.

Mead Island, at an elevation of around 787 feet above sea level, would disappear once the lake had exceeded a height of sixteen feet above the

Conklingville Dam spillway. Other islands, such as Deer, Sand, Beacon, the Kenyon Group, and so on, would probably disappear in close unison.

The last island to vanish would likely be Scout Island, which is somewhat over 800 feet above sea level. By the time that Scout Island became totally submerged, a majority of camps and cottages near the water's edge would be either completely under water or partially submerged. Those spared would be homes on lofty embankments, particularly camps located on the opposite side of roadways from the lake.

Northampton Beach, due to its flatness, would be totally gone by the time the lake height had exceeded nine feet above the Conklingville Dam spillway. The village of Cranberry Creek would be under water by the time the lake had crested to 786 feet. Fish House would vanish during this stage, as well as the lower section of Sacandaga Park.

By the time the Sac had risen to over 800 feet above sea level, no islands would be left, and the lake would be well over twenty-nine feet above its maximum carrying capacity. The volume of the lake would have increased tremendously since not only its height, but surface area as well, would have grown as new shoreline was captured.

Northville would still be above waterline, but instead of seemingly being perched on a plateau with cliff-like walls leading to the lake, it would be virtually at the water's edge. Broadalbin would probably remain pretty much unaffected, but Vail Mills, due to its proximity to the Kennyetto Creek, might not fair as well.

The lower part of Batchellerville would be gone, as well as the tip of Sinclair Point and significant parts of Mayfield.

Twenty-nine feet of increased elevation, then, would make a significant difference to many of the homeowners and communities around the lake. However, in many respects, the lake would still look much like it currently does, minus the islands. The deepest part of the reservoir would increase to ninety-nine feet; the waters by Batchellerville to around seventy-four feet; and the waters around Northville to fifty-nine feet.

The shoreline of the Great Sacandaga Lake would increase beyond 125 miles, but probably not as much as you would imagine. The maximum width of the lake would also increase beyond its present 28,000 feet, but once again, not necessarily in a dramatic fashion. The reason for these changes being insubstantial has to do with the way the valley is laid out. The GSL already occupies all of the flat areas. Although the lake may rise twenty-nine feet higher, there is not a lot of horizontal direction to move out into since the walls of the valley become steeper the further out you push.

Assuming that the water level was never brought down to pre-earthquake elevations— a very unlikely prospect—humans would adapt just as Cro-Magnon man did before the advancing and retreating glaciers. In this case, new homes would sprout up, new roads would be built, and life would go on. This is not only the way of the Sacandaga Valley, which has already gone through one major topological transformation in recent memory, but the way of the human race.

NIGHT OF THE 80-MPH WINDS

WHEN THE MICROBURST OF 1995 HIT, ALL HELL BROKE LOOSE

This incredible experience shows just how thrilling and unpredictable living on the Great Sacandaga Lake can be. My wife and I own a year-round camp near Diamond Point on the South Shore Road, several miles above North Broadalbin, and it faces across five miles of lake waters almost directly to the shores of Cranberry Creek.

For almost anyone in the greater part of New York State, the date Saturday, July 15th, 1995 will not soon be forgotten. It was during the early morning hours on Saturday that storm winds achieved a velocity of 77 mph as measured by the National Weather Service at the Albany County airport—stronger than ever recorded before in the capital region except for November of 1950.

The preceding day, Friday, had produced a record breaking high of 98°, and virtually anyone who had a swimming pool, access to a lake, or reliable air conditioning, had taken off to their favorite retreat. As you can imagine, the two of us were enjoying cooling off at the lake. That night, we had gone to bed with all of the windows thrown wide open, and the bedroom floor fan revved up to full throttle; without a gentle breeze to bring in the cooling air from the lake, the temperature indoors had stayed well into the high 80's. Fitfully, we dozed off to sleep.

Around 6:10 A.M., I was suddenly awakened by an ominous feeling that something wasn't quite right. I realized immediately that it was the sound of the fan coming to an abrupt halt that had awakened me; a quick glance at my unlit clock revealed that the power had gone off. But something else had also caught my attention—the sound of howling wind.

Wondering if a severe electrical storm had knocked out the power around us, I jumped out of bed and dashed into the living room, where two large sliding glass doors overlook the lake. In the early morning light that was rapidly dimming, I could see trees and bushes swaying wildly in the wind. Rain was beginning to fall, and it was obvious that a storm was rushing at us. Quickly I closed the sliding doors.

As I continued to stare at the landscape, the wind picked up to a velocity I had never seen before. Pellets of rain suddenly began flying horizontal to the ground. The whole quality of light around the camp and lake altered as though polarized. With one great whoosh, the wind increased still further, and suddenly lawn chairs and everything not attached to the deck beyond the glass doors got sucked off the porch and sent flying into the sky.

"Honey! Come quick!" I called out to Barbara, with some anxiety in my voice. "What's happening is unbelievable. You've got to see this!"

By now the wind was thundering over the camp like a raging river (which some people later likened to the sound of a thundering train), the windows were rattling, and a whistling sound could be heard emanating from every joint in the house as wind tried to force its way through. Almost immediately, Barbara was next to my side. We both stared out anxiously through the glass doors, feeling more helpless and uneasy as the wind's ferocity kept increasing.

"This is starting to get scary!" I shouted, concerned that the structural limits of wood and lumber might be exceeded if the winds kept pressing in.

Just then, a huge tree limb some eighteen inches thick and twenty-five feet long came crashing down onto the deck and roof of the house, right in front of where we were standing! Another foot or two and the branches would have crashed through the glass panes and struck us.

We didn't need any prompting. "Let's get out of here!" Barbara shouted and we quickly retreated to the front of the house, which seemed safer because it was further away from the battering ram of attacking wind.

We huddled together, wondering what was going to happen next. Fortunately, the wind all at once began to diminish and within a moment or two, the worst was over.

Barbara gave a sigh of relief.

From our front porch windows, we could see lawn furniture and tree limbs laying all about the road as if scattered by a giant petulant child. Evidence of the storm's fury was everywhere.

"What about our boat?" I asked. We scurried to the back of the house which faces the lake and, looking past the huge branch that had fallen, could see that the lake was churning and tossing like the ocean. Still, none of the boats moored out from shore looked any the worse for wear. Not so for the boats inland, however. Our fifty pound, twelve foot aluminum rowboat had been completely flipped over, and a neighbor's boat had been tossed right off of its trailer.

We stared out the window for a while, mesmerized by how the storm had transformed the landscape. Since lightning was crackling everywhere in the sky, and rolls of thunder boomed incessantly across the valley, I waited a while before going outside to retrieve our scattered lawn chairs.

Later in the morning, my neighbor to the north of me, David, brought over his gas-driven chain saw and we made quick work of the huge tree limb. Earlier, I had made the discovery that my electric chain saw wouldn't work because the power was still off.

I learned that my neighbor to the south, Bob, and his family had been peacefully sleeping outside on their porch deck when the storm hit. They ran inside quickly, but as fast as they scrambled, the storm moved even faster. It came roaring into their house, scattering things every which way, before they could board up all the windows. A neighbor across the street from us reported that a huge tree limb just narrowly missed his house; and so it went, tale after tale, for many of the people around the Sacandaga area.

Others in the capital region, unfortunately, were not as lucky. A 72-year-old woman in Westerlo was struck by a tree after getting out of her car to clear away an obstruction. In Lake Luzerne, at the Lake George KOA campground, a trailer was crushed with three people inside: the woman was killed instantly, her husband suffered a fractured skull, and their granddaughter was critically injured. To the north, at Lake Lila in the town on Long Lake, a couple in their tent was struck by a falling tree. The wife was killed outright, and the husband suffered a concussion. Similarly, a family camping out at Eighth Lake was struck by a crashing tree. The man was killed, and his family injured seriously enough to be hospitalized. By comparison, I felt lucky ... and grateful.

How severe was the storm in terms of inconvenience? Well, 230,000 Niagara Mohawk customers lost power statewide, and a few had to wait days to have it restored. Some likened the effects of the storm to the freak snow squall in October of 1987 that dropped nineteen inches of heavy snow on the region, and knocked down power lines for miles around.

All in all, this was a storm of unusual power and ferocity; one which even most elders were hard pressed to recall ever experiencing before. For a moment or two, it was as if parts of New York State had been transported to the top of Mount Washington in New Hampshire, where winds exceed hurricane force (75 mph) on an average of 104 days per year (and where, I might add, the highest wind velocity on earth—231 mph—was recorded in 1934). Meteorologists later called the storm a "bomb"—the result of a "mesoscale convective complex," where a rare combination of excessively high temperatures and humidity levels produces weather of unusual severity.

All I know is that the images of the onrushing storm and crashing tree limb right in front of me will live on in my mind forever; another reminder that there are adventures at the Great Sacandaga Lake both for people who seek them out and for those who don't!

Going to Bat for Bats

Believe it or not, bats may be one of man's best friends

One of my first impressions of the Great Sacandaga Lake was walking down by the shore in front of the Sacandaga Trailer Park at dusk with Barbara, watching the waters growing red and then dissolving into deep grays of silver as the sun slowly sank behind the west shore mountains. As we walked along, all at once I heard the sounds of swooping and rustling coming from above us. I looked up and saw a blur of motion.

"What was that?" I asked, having caught a fleeting glimpse of something bird-like.

"A bat," Barbara replied nonchalantly.

"A bat?" I answered with some surprise. Then, "Oh. That's cool." And with that, we continued on walking without further comment.

But, later, that incident got me to thinking: Bats are so useful and ecologically important, yet they are terribly misunderstood. In our outings over the years, Barbara and I have explored a number of caves in the Adirondacks, Helderbergs, and Catskills. In the process we have also seen our fair share of bats. While exploring one Schoharie County cave in particular, known as Gage's Cave (or Balls Cave), we crawled into a huge underground chamber called the *Amphitheater*, and observed hundreds of bats hanging from the ceiling over our heads. It was quite a sight to behold.

And no, the bats didn't swoop down from their perches, ending up tangling themselves in our clothes and hair; nor did they flash formidable incisors and, like vampires of legend, display an appetite for blood.

The fact of the matter is that bats, almost without exception, are gentle, peace-loving creatures who want nothing more than to avoid contact with humans; and this they are able to do with great aplomb. Bats employ sonar for navigating, particularly in pitch-black caves and, contrary to popular belief, also possess fairly good vision (they can see us very well, thank you). For these two reasons, bats have absolutely no difficulty keeping out of your hair and clothing. What's more, except for a few species of bats found in the tropics, none feast on blood nor have any desire to do so. Generally, bats like to snack on precisely the kinds of vermin that humans strenuously try to avoid—mosquitoes, black flies, and other assorted flying insects with nasty reputations. While we're debunking myths, I suppose it's also worth mentioning that it is a rare bat that you'll encounter who is rabid.

That's why, as we walked along the shore listening to the periodic flapping of tiny wings above us, I couldn't help but thinking friendly and positive thoughts about bats. For here were the bats, like tiny guardian angels above us, sweeping the air free of insects as we strolled along. Realizing that one good turn deserves another, I decided it was high time to give bats some good press; to encourage their acceptance in the community as the benign and beneficial creatures they are in real life—not the crazed and terrifying demons of the night they are often portrayed as being. Unfortunately, there are many people, armed with superstition and fear, who would rather greet bats with baseball bats than open arms.

Let's verbally bat the subject of bats around a bit then. To begin, in order for any species to survive, there must be suitable habitation as well as opportunities for foraging. Unfortunately, the Sacandaga Valley lacks caves, one of the principal dwelling places used by bats. At best, there may be a talus cave or two in the area formed when a bunch of rocks pile up, but talus caves generally are shallow and provide meager accommodations for most bats.

I know of at least one bat that dwells under the shingles of my woodshed, so I can easily imagine that bats, being opportunistic, might occupy an unused attic, belfry, deserted building, or old ruin. Indeed, I would suspect that these types of dwellings are the prominent habitats for bats locally. Unless humans are in close association with such habitats, the bats are typically left undisturbed and coexistence is achieved. When humans are in close association, however, then someone ultimately has to vacate the premises, and usually it is the bat that is forced to concede territory. But not always. Sometimes the bats persevere and win out. Undoubtedly, the term "bats in your belfry" arose when an occasional human was driven crazy by the eerie sounds of bats in the upstairs attic.

The main problem with having bats in your attic is that they emit high-pitch squeals, make a lot of scraping noises, and scare a lot of people with their antics. Just as a point of illustration, I once had a bat dive-bomb me in a cave. Presumably, it was feeling trapped between me and the end of the passageway I was approaching. Let me tell you, meeting an excited bat face to face can be a scary experience (probably for the bat, too). To be honest, as much as I like bats, I wouldn't necessarily want them living in my attic either, not only because of the noise, but for other good reasons. Bats produce guano (bat droppings) which can breed diseases, and which will cause a noticeable smell if enough bats occupy a particular dwelling for a sufficient length of time.

For this reason, Barbara and I have casually talked about putting up a "bat house" in the back yard. Such a dwelling is nothing more than a bird house specifically designed for bats. The bat house would provide lodging for one or more bats and ensure their presence in the immediate vicinity. It would also, hopefully, provide a habitat that would always remain more suitable than my attic. The bats, in turn, would earn their keep by reducing the number of flying insects in the yard, consuming about half their weight each evening unless they are in hibernation.

A couple of bats patrolling the area, hence, could accomplish far more in terms of pest control than three pounds of pesticide sprays, and would certainly be less irritating and obnoxious than chemical repellents. In the era of threats from mosquito-born diseases such as the West Nile virus, this is an attractive alternative.

Lest you think that I have gone totally batty, the answer is "no" to the question you're thinking. Barbara and I have not built a bat house. Still, when you think about it the next time a dark cloud of mosquitoes and black flies descend upon you, having a bat for a neighbor might not be such a bad idea.

WATER, WATER EVERYWHERE

ALTHOUGH WATER SEEMS TO BE EVERYWHERE, HOW MUCH IS ACTUALLY DRINKABLE?

The Great Sacandaga Lake, at its fullest, contains 283 billion gallons of water, and yet none of it is conserved for drinking as it is in some reservoirs. Rather, the lake waters are released for power generation, to flush out the Hudson River when salty sea water begins to intrude upstream, and to provide a holding tank in early spring so that the Sacandaga River, a main tributary to the Hudson River, can be confined, thus preventing the Hudson River from becoming too energetic.

But will this always remain so? Might there not come a time when the waters of the Great Sacandaga Lake will be coveted as a drinking source, and not just as a flush tank?

At first glance, it's easy to be forgiven for thinking that water is the most prevalent and available of all molecules on the Earth. After all, 70% of the planet is covered with water, and that amounts to 1,280,000,000 cubic kilometers. However, almost all of this water, except for a measly 2.6%, is contained in the Earth's oceans where the presence of salt makes it unfit for human consumption or the irrigation of lands.

Still, 2.6% amounts to 337,000 cubic kilometers of fresh water, and that's a great deal of available fluid. But is it really available?

To be sure, water doesn't exist only as a liquid. It can also be found in its gaseous and solid states. As it turns out, 98% of all fresh water is locked up in the polar regions as ice, or on top of Earth's mountains as snow. Furthermore, another 1/30,000 of Earth's water is contained, at any moment, in the atmosphere as water vapor, making it unavailable until it rains. This means, then, that a mere 1/20th of 1% of all water on the Earth is in an available, fresh water, liquid form.

But that's not all. Some of this water is located deep under the planet's surface as ground water and not always so easily extracted. This is particularly true in regions which are relatively desiccated. Then, on the opposite hand, there are regions where mighty rivers can be found, such as the Amazon in South America, but which are located in areas unfrequented by humans; thus, prodigious amounts of water end up flowing across thousands of miles of land, but with little of it ever being consumed in the process.

Only the tiniest fraction of Earth's water, then, is contained in a form that is drinkable, and located near centers of population where it can be readily consumed. Which leads us back to the Great Sacandaga Lake. Here, we find that the waters of the GSL are fairly pure, and can be drunk at will without any initial preparation or filtering. This does not mean that all is necessarily well, however. A sizable number of existing camps were built during a time between the '30s and '50s when environmental codes were not quite as strict, and thus inadequate or antiquated septic systems have been grandfathered in. There is still pollution entering the lake in some quantity.

Then there's the matter of gasoline and motor oil spillage from boats and jet skis. As more boats proliferate on the lake, particularly jet skis, the buildup of spills increases. According to one source, two stroke engines from personal watercrafts, such as jet skis, discharge up to one-third of their fuel-oil mixture into the water.

Fortunately, the Great Sacandaga Lake is not a static, unchanging body of water with no inlet or outlet. There are a number of tributaries entering the lake, including the Sacandaga River, its main source of water. And because the lake is a reservoir, with huge releases of water made on a seasonal basis, any significant build-up of pollution is expelled as well.

Water is a renewable resource, but it still requires careful and planned conservation. Already in some parts of the country the amount of ground water pumped out from the depths of the Earth has exceeded the volume of water percolating back down from rainfall. Clearly, if this problem were to occur in the northeast, perhaps through several seasons of inordinately small rainfall, then alternate sources of water, such as the Sac, would suddenly assume greater importance.

It behooves us, then, to maintain the purity of the lake waters, for both esthetic and pragmatic reasons, and to loudly protest when we see somebody carelessly or thoughtlessly polluting them.

PERSONAL SUBMERSIBLES

MAKE ROOM FOR CAPTAIN NEMO, FOLKS

I was talking with a friend recently, and somehow the question arose as to what boating on the Great Sacandaga Lake might look like in the future. Obviously, over the previous seven decades, the boating character of the lake has changed rather significantly from sailboats, rowboats, and canoes to motorized craft; from small vessels to large party barges; from boats traveling at low velocities to recreational vehicles capable of tremendous speeds; from propeller driven vessels to jet-powered crafts; and from moderate sized boats designed for carrying a small family to extremely mobile and personalized crafts for one or two—jet skies, the modern equivalent, I would suppose, of the cowboy and his horse.

But where to next? On a body of water such as the GSL, boats can only get so big and so fast. Obviously, the limits for expansion have already been reached or are fast approaching; and in terms of versatility, it's hard to imagine any craft more fluid and responsive than a jet ski. Perhaps, then, there is little left in the shape of things to come, and the Great Sacandaga Lake of tomorrow will look pretty much as it does today.

But don't you believe it for a moment!

There are still untapped areas for expansion, and sooner or later someone will begin exploiting the potentials for these new frontiers; and if it can't be on the water's surface, then it will be down below! Welcome to the world of the "personal submersible."

Imagine a tiny one—or two—person submarine, jet-powered, that you can jump into and, with absolutely no fuss, immediately dive below the lake's surface to explore the depths. Imagine also a set of onboard instruments that allow you to instantaneously know the position and altitude of all other crafts on the lake, both above and below the water's surface. Obviously, it would not bode well to come rising up to the surface, only to discover a 50-mph speedboat bearing down on you.

These personal submersibles of the future will be highly maneuverable, although not to the same extent as a jet ski since water is considerably more viscous than air. They will also be extremely safe, perhaps even foolproof, if there ever is such a thing, so that no human could become trapped at the bottom of the lake or drowned by a sudden deluge of incoming water. Assuming that these conditions can be met in the future, the personal submersible would open up a whole new realm of adventure to boaters—the world of deep-water exploration.

Naturally, at the Great Sacandaga Lake, there is no need to worry about diving too deep and being crushed by the water's pressure, which increases directly as a function of depth. At its deepest, near the original river channel, the waters of the GSL go no further down than seventy-five feet. Still, that is a fairly respectable depth, and over twice that from which divers would undergo decompression if they were to spend any significant time at the bottom.

The problem with the Sacandaga Reservoir, however, is that there is little to see once you're under its surface. Looking through the window of your submarine, essentially all you will observe in front of you are vast deserts of sand and mud, cities of rocks, lots of tree stumps, and an occasional clump of weeds, but little else. To be sure, some traces of the pre-reservoir days remain in the form of old foundations, but these are far and few between and becoming increasingly dissipated by the water's erosive action. What's more, like all cold water lakes in the Northeastern United States, the GSL tends to be dark and murky, and contains fish of generally dull and unexciting colors. All of this adds up to a very unappealing visual experience.

As a result, it seems likely that even in the future—if and when the personal submersible becomes a reality—there will be few lake-users owning one, much less using one. If the personal submersible ends up being set into motion, it will probably be in tow behind someone's car as they head down to the southern United States where the waters are more tropical and contain something to actually see.

THE GREAT SACANDAGA LAKE IN THE YEAR 2070

PUT THIS ARTICLE INTO A TIME CAPSULE AND OPEN IT SEVENTY YEARS FROM NOW. I BET I'M MORE WRONG THAN RIGHT, BUT HEY—THAT'S THE BATTING AVERAGE FOR ALL FUTURISTS!

What will life be like seventy years from now at the Great Sacandaga Lake? With the reader's indulgence, I would like to make several predictions.

"But why seventy years from now?" you might ask. The reason is that seventy years happens to be the interval of time that has elapsed (from the time that this article was written) since the Conklingville Dam permanently interrupted the flow of the Sacandaga River; and seventy years is a pretty significant length of time.

Just imagine what life was like in the year 1860—seventy years before the GSL was created. At that time, the Sacandaga Valley was inhabited by a collection of 'rough and tumble' frontier towns containing a variety of lumber mills, tanneries, and glove factories. In 1860, the boom town of Batchellerville had only been in existence for twenty-three years.

There was no Sacandaga Park. That wouldn't come until 1875, when the railroad connecting Fonda, Johnstown, and Gloversville was extended to Northville, making possible the mass transportation of people and, ultimately, the creation of an amusement park just south of Northville.

Certainly there was no thought whatsoever of a dam being built and the valley flooded. For this reason, a futurist like myself making predictions in the year 1860 would have overlooked the most important change of all that would be wrought on the Sacandaga Valley—namely, it's flooding.

I say this only to show how difficult foretelling the future is, and how easy—in fact, likely—it is to slip on an unforeseen banana. Quite honestly, the odds are more likely that I am to be gloriously wrong than gloriously right. Still, the fun is in making the predictions; and, after all, how many people old enough to read this article are going to be around seventy years from now to berate me if my predictions go totally off the mark?

Ideally, this chapter should be put into a time capsule so that future readers can enjoy a good laugh.

Okay. Onward now to the year 2070—seventy years into the future. . . . There are ten predictions that I would like to make:

FIRST of all, the Great Sacandaga Lake will most assuredly become more and more prized as a source of fresh water, with consideration given as to how these waters can be better conserved and used for human consumption, as opposed to being unceremoniously released to flush out the Hudson River, and drive a few more turbines along the river banks (although these are both very good and noble purposes for the Sacandaga waters at present).

The fact is that the amount of fresh water on Earth is rapidly dwindling. Although three-fourths of Earth is water, making the name of this planet rather a misnomer, most of Earth's water is contained in its vast, salty oceans (totally undrinkable), and locked up in the form of ice in its polar regions (totally unreachable). Only a tiny fraction of Earth's water, perhaps one percent at best, is contained in its lakes, rivers, and ground water deposits.

The lakes and rivers are at various stages of undrinkability, leaving only small amounts of ground water for human consumption and irrigation, and these are being siphoned off more quickly than they can be replenished.

The Great Sacandaga Lake, then, has something of value in the future—namely, a repository for drinking water.

SECOND, Northville and Broadalbin, the two main towns situated virtually at opposite ends of the lake, will go through a period of significant revival and prominence, increasing both in population and business. This will occur as both towns play up their unique histories.

No doubt the revival will be related to tourism, and there will be additional hotels, motels, and bed & breakfasts, like the *Inn at the Bridge* in Northville, around the lake.

Hopefully, the development of additional tourist attractions and businesses will not degrade into gaudiness, flooding the area with fast food chains and trinket shops. My guess is that the Sacandaga towns and villages will do everything in their power to preserve their heritage and rustic beauty.

Although both towns will grow, my prediction is that Northville will grow faster and remain larger than Broadalbin, fueled primarily by its proximity to the lake and greater centrality within the Adirondack Park.

THIRD, the lake's perimeter will experience a few significant modifications. So far, most of the lakefront is owned and inhabited by people living in small cottages and summer homes. What I see happening in years to come is the consolidation of some properties, and the creation of one or two hotels or resorts, unless such development is forever zoned against. Such lodgings might be tolerated since they would bring increased tourism to the area, allowing local businesses to prosper and flourish.

FOURTH, the Great Sacandaga Lake will increasingly become an area attractive to tourists not only because of its lake, but because of its unique history as a valley transformed into a lake-oriented community. Already there are vibrant historical societies in Broadalbin, Edinburg, Northville-Northampton, Mayfield, and elsewhere, preserving and promoting the history of the area.

Within time, it is my prediction that there will be greater unification of these historical societies, so that the history of the GSL and its various parts will be interwoven into one tapestry.

FIFTH, the Hudson River-Black River Regulating District will increasingly give higher priority to the recreational needs of the area (and, indeed, in the year 2000, some changes have already started). These changes will continue as more and more people move into the area, and the demands of tourism slowly override those that were the prominent ones for the lake's creation in the past.

SIXTH, the Great Sacandaga Lake will become more and more populated by motorized craft. No doubt there will be huge outcries at some point about the prospect of the Sac becoming another Lake George, where 9,000 boats can be seen out on the lake on a given weekend day, and also the rising volume of lake noise pollution. Although I predict a backlash against motorized boats someday, I also believe that the motorboat proponents will win out, at least at the GSL. Too many people utilize power craft, and have too much money invested in their equipment to willingly agree to cut back on, or eliminate, an insatiable need for power and speed.

Barbara's prediction, contrary to mine, is that the noise level will decrease, providing (always provisionally, of course) that alternate forms of energy are discovered and utilized, such as solar power. A jet ski running on solar power, for example, would produce a fraction of the noise it currently generates, and would therefore be that less objectionable.

My prediction, nevertheless, is that the lake will continue to grow noisier, with only one possible factor reversing this grim trend: If the day comes when the lake water must be preserved for its purity, then a proliferation of motorized craft may be prohibited due to their inevitable discharge of gasoline and oil into the lake.

SEVENTH, I predict that a huge amusement park, similar to the entertainment area that once existed at Sacandaga Park, will be constructed to further promote tourism in the area.

Assuming that this prediction comes to pass, the Great Sacandaga Lake will be altered significantly and permanently, and not necessarily in keeping with its developing history, although, then again, Sacandaga Park—the Coney Island of the Adirondacks—did once exist south of Northville.

EIGHTH, the property values on the lake will continue to increase dramatically, and why not? With population expansion and a finite number of accessible lakes, it's only inevitable that lakefront property will increase in value, with the public clamoring for more and more. Although New York State is blessed with an unusually large number of lakes, the accessible ones are already heavily utilized, and the remaining ones are either too remote, too tiny, or too undesirable for other reasons (such as bogginess, acid rain levels, and so on).

NINTH, the lake will go through a period of foolishness when a lake monster is sighted, and a flock of additional reports follow. Scotland, of course, has its famous Loch Ness Monster, "Nessie." Lake Champlain and Lake George also have their fresh water monsters. Lake Champlain's sea monster is affectionately called "Champy"—supposedly first seen by Samuel de Champlain in July of 1609—and in 1980 the Village of Port Henry went so far as to decree that "all the waters of Lake Champlain which adjoin the Village of Port Henry are hereby declared off limits to anyone who would in any way harm, harass, or destroy the Lake Champlain Sea Monster." Lake George's sea monster is known simply as "George."

In *Days Past*, by Town of Day historian Nancy S. Morris, Don Bowman jokingly talks about "Saxie the Mermaid"—the GSL's sea monster.

We all know, however, that sightings of lake monsters can often be simply outright deceptions. Silver Lake in western New York, for instance, went through a well played-out lake monster hoax in 1855, which just goes to show that such sightings are not merely the recent manifestation of New Age thinking and our love affairs with UFO's, Bigfoot, and things that go bump in the night.

With interest in dinosaurs at an all-time high, it is inevitable that a water serpent of some kind will be seen by supposedly "reliable" observers, leaving the Great Sacandaga Lake to bask in its new-found glory for a while. No doubt some skeptics will ultimately ask the discerning question: Where did a prehistoric lake monster come from if the Sacandaga Reservoir has only existed since 1930?

TENTH, a wind-powered generator will be put up on the east or west side of the lake, presumably on top of one of the windiest hills, in order to generate electricity. Except for hydropower, can you ask for a cleaner source of energy?

And there you have it—my list of predictions for the year 2070.

LIVING ON A RESERVOIR

THE UPS AND DOWNS OF LIVING ON A LAKE THAT REFUSES TO STAY PUT

Whenever an article on the Great Sacandaga Lake appears and mention is made that the water level varies seasonally, the author of the piece inevitably adopts a sympathetic tone, commiserating with lake-users who are pictured standing by helplessly as the water level goes up and down like a yo-yo. In this worst case scenario beaches lengthen, turn muddy, and recede further from lakefront homes; incautious boaters begin damaging or losing motorboat props on submerged shoals that are now close to the surface; and fish begin dying off in greater numbers, making the lake less fishable to sports-minded people.

While all of these points are true and cause the two of us—along with many other residents—endless frustrations, I believe that there are still advantages to living at the edge of a reservoir. In fact, significant advantages!

When I first suggested this premise to Barbara, she looked at me dubiously for a long time, and finally said, "Well, I can't wait to hear what you've come up with."

Unlike Barbara, I won't make you wait a minute longer. Here, for better or worse, are the advantages to living on a reservoir.

To begin, a substantial volume of old lake water gets released on a yearly basis in order to make room for spring's snowmelt. Now, I'm not a hydrologist or chemist, but it seems reasonable to me that the waters of the GSL are unusually pure precisely because they are replenished constantly. The same water simply doesn't stay in the reservoir long enough to stagnate and serve as a breeding ground for slime, algae, and other biological materials that might make the water less fit to drink. Even in the shallow lowlands the lake doesn't become particularly swampy. What's more, the receding shoreline exposes underwater plants to winter's austerities, killing off large numbers before they can proliferate.

Purity, then, is a significant advantage, and it is psychologically comforting to know that if you accidentally gulp down a mouthful of lake water while swimming, you're not likely to get a stomach full of bad microbes.

Then there's the matter of island destinations for exploration. The lake possesses a variety of tiny islands: some, Scout Island and Beacon, for example, are down near the southern end of the lake; others, Mead Island and the Kenyon Group, to cite a few, are located near the northwestern part of the lake past Sinclair Point.

Between these two clusters of islands, however, are miles of expansive nothingness—a fact I am well aware of since Barbara and I live next to Diamond Point, which faces out across miles and miles of broad water. From our cottage, the closest island is Sand Island, which is roughly one and a third miles away going southwest; the next closest is a small bar-like island off of Sinclair Point, some two miles or more distant to the northwest. Straight across there is nothing…

…Nothing, that is, until the lake level begins to drop. Suddenly, shoals well hidden under the lake magically begin to appear. In the article *Island Hopping* I talk about how Barbara and I make use of these surfacing shoals as destinations to which we canoe and kayak.

What's significant here is that these shoals only surface when the water level drops appreciably. Should the height of the reservoir remain fairly constant, we would have no nearby islands and shoals to explore, and the lake would become infinitely less intimate and accessible to us. The dropping water level, then, provides the advantage of new places to visit and explore, and to use as stepping stones for more distant explorations.

Then there's the matter of shorefront erosion. In the early part of spring, when the water is at its highest, shore fronts, including our own, take quite a beating. Recently, I couldn't help but notice how the pounding waves had rearranged huge rocks in front of our cottage, even eroding away precious topsoil. Naturally, we weren't happy about the damage inflicted as the lake decided to ripple its brawny muscles.

However, when the water level begins falling, the shore line moves away from the rocky property edges. When huge waves subsequently come crashing in, they merely wash up on the expanding beach, and do absolutely no damage to the property beyond.

The variable water level, then, lessens the impact of the lake on the containing land. The receding waters even allow lakefront owners to rebuild their rock barriers, with the permission and good graces of the Hudson River-Black River Regulating District, of course.

Finally, the lengthening beach front is not necessarily all bad. Although it means that you have to walk a further distance to get to the lake, it also means that you have more beach to utilize and play on, and at no additional cost. A number of summers ago, there was so much exposed beach that we could have put a football field on it! Extra land, then, means extra potential for fun.

So there you have it. Although the variable water level will inevitably cause its share of problems and frustrations to lake users, there are advantages, too. As for me, I'd rather see the glass or, in this case, the lake, half full than half empty.

SKIJAKING ON THE SACANDAGA

**WARNING! THIS IS NOT AN ARTICLE ON JET SKIS!
BUT DON'T LET THAT STOP YOU FROM READING ON**

Most folks are used to seeing a variety of boats of all shapes and sizes when they scan the blue horizon for sailing crafts. But I bet few here have seen anybody whizzing along on a pair of skijaks.

Skijaks?!

That's exactly what the two of us first exclaimed to each other when we came across the strange and fascinating sport of skijaking, pronounced "ski-yak-ing." We had looked at an advertisement in a local newspaper and read the following unforgettable caption: "*Learn to skijak in one hour and be the first on your lake to walk on water*."

"What do you think?" I asked Barbara. The idea of walking on water had a real intriguing sound to it. I was finally going to have a religious experience.

"May the force be with you," Barbara replied with mock seriousness. "But you'll get no groveling and bowing from me unless you're walking on the Sea of Galilee."

(Right!)

Now that I had decided to go for it, just what was skijaking anyhow? How do you go about learning the art of walking on water?

To begin, I realized very quickly that skijaking is no ordinary sport. It is, for lack of a better word, a *hybrid*. Just as a mule is a cross between a mare and a male donkey, so skijaking is a cross between skiing and kayaking. It's like cross-country skiing, only you use kayaks instead of skis, and a double bladed paddle instead of poles.

Because of this, skijaking is neither for hee-haw-ers nor ya-hoo-ers. Skijaking is for....well.... someone who likes to try something a little off the beaten path.

My first experience with skijaking took place in the summer of '91 and, happily, right up at the Sac. With much bravado, as I attempted to mask my underlying insecurities, I stepped into two narrow, eleven-foot-long kayaks (one for each foot) and, grabbing hold of a ten foot, double-bladed paddle, began propelling myself across the water using the diagonal stride common to cross-country skiing.

My first attempt produced immediate and striking results; I toppled headfirst into the water and came up sputtering. Well, no one said it was going to be easy.

"Bravo!" Barbara yelled out gleefully, sitting in a canvass-backed beach chair on the shore with a cold drink in her hand, and all the comforts of someone not on skijaks. "Do it again!"

Obviously, I was destined to be her afternoon's entertainment.

But after getting upright again, I stayed up for good, and learned how to do a diagonal stride on water instead of snow. And I've been going strong ever since.

According to Barbara, I've become the Sacandaga version of King of the Mountain. I've crested three-foot waves, had jet skiers use me as a buoy for making power turns, and once even narrowly escaped a lightning strike; but no one has yet toppled me, although I'm convinced that some, including mother nature, have tried their best to do just that!

The fun part of skijaking, besides getting wind, sun, and water in abundance, is watching people's jaws drop as they see you strolling across the water up to them, seemingly contradicting all known laws of nature, not to mention the laws of the Great Sacandaga Lake.

And in case you're wondering, no one has yet bowed down after seeing me walk across water towards them. I guess my wife was right about that. People just aren't as impressed by quasi-miracles as they were 2,000 years ago.

The reason I bring up the subject of skijaking in the first place is that it allows the adventurous soul an opportunity for exploring the GSL in a nontraditional way. How so? Well, you can travel through water so shallow that you'd almost swear there was only water vapor under the skijaks. On one occasion, Barbara was in the kayak and I was on the skijaks. Suddenly we hit some shoals. Guess who got stuck!

Secondly, you can really see for a long distance when you skijak. After all, it's necessary that you stand upright. This gives you a distinct height advantage over a person sitting in a canoe or kayak.

The only disadvantage in standing upright is when you encounter heavy winds. On skijaks, heading into a stiff wind can make you feel like you're trying to go forward in a wind tunnel.

Last but not least, skijaking is an attention-getter. People are naturally curious about who you are ("Did you come from Mars?") and just what you're doing with pontoons on your feet ("Did your kayak break in two?").

Some of the onlookers will even want to take a stab at it themselves. Naturally, it's next to impossible for any first timer to maintain his or her balance, or to move with convincing speed; consequently, my meager abilities, by contrast, look all the more impressive to those who aren't taking this factor into consideration.

But best of all, the group of onlookers usually generates at least one attractive, impressionable, young woman who steps forward and asks for personal instruction. My wife, however, always seems to be present, and is guaranteed to throw cold water on such sporting propositions.

During the nine years I have been skijaking, there have been times when I ventured out two or three miles from shore, always with some trepidation. Although I know how to remount the skijaks if I should fall in, there's still the matter of weather conditions. If the lake is choppy and foaming at the mouth, getting back up may be next to impossible, and I may find myself wishing that I had taken more lessons on riding the mechanical bull during the heyday of disco.

For the time being, though, all is well in the world of cross-water skijaking.

SACANDAGA BY WINTER

WHEN WINTER COMES, ICE TENACIOUSLY FORMS, SPREADING A THICK PROTECTIVE LAYER ACROSS THE TUNDRA OF THE LAKE, SEPARATING FISH FROM MAN. SNOW FILLS THE WOODLANDS, AND MOUNTAIN PEAKS TURN SILVER, SPARKLING LIKE DIAMONDS UNDER THE BRIGHT SOLSTICE MOON. WINDOWS GET FROSTY, AND THE FRAGRANT SMELL OF WOOD-BURNING STOVES AND FIREPLACES PERMEATES THE AIR

Winter is a wonderful time to be up at the GSL, for it is a world vastly different from the blue skies and green grasses of summer. It is a world of snow and ice, and skeletal trees overlooking a frozen, motionless lake.

To be sure, the topography of the Sac has changed significantly in the months since summer. By midwinter, the water level has dropped to an all-season low, and shoals and islands have reached their maximum height above the water line. Rock Island, for instance—an underwater shoal that remains submerged until the end of summer—is now a lofty 20-foot-high hillock.

Although the entire lake is frozen solid by January, the ice is by no means uniformly flat. It has been shaped and contoured by the land masses beneath it, and bulges here and there. Shoals that rise above the water, and islands that have expanded in size and height, now loom like hills over the otherwise flat terrain.

The fact that the lake is a reservoir can produce some unusual phenomenon. On our very first winter visit, we were puzzled by a number of foot high mounds that were scattered about on top of the ice, generally within several hundred feet of the shoreline. From a distance, they looked like giant pods that had opened and disgorged something (much like the sinister husks in the movie *Alien*, if one were to let one's imagination run free). Upon closer examination, however, it became evident to us that these strangely formed upthrustings of ice and snow were actually mounds raised above the ice-line by underlying tree stumps.

"I get it," Barbara said at last. "When ice first forms on the lake, the tree stumps are under water. Then, as water continues to be released from the lake, the ice sheet drops, breaking apart when it lands on top of an exposed tree stump."

"Good deduction, mon ami," I said, trying my best to sound like Hercule Poirot (the Agatha Christie Belgian detective). "And that explains why there are so many mounds around Stump Island and the other nearby shoals."

At the rate things are going, however, it is unlikely that many stumps will remain within a short span of time. Every year during the spring, hundreds more lose their precarious hold on the sandy ground, and pop up to the surface like giant corks. Usually, we see one or two each year washed up along the beach near Diamond Point.

As we walked across the vast expanse of the ice, we couldn't help but feel small and insignificant, totally dwarfed by the hills around us and the whiteness of ice and clouds that seamlessly merged at the horizon. We had no problem, however, finding a path to traverse. A myriad of snowmobile tracks crisscrossed the lake, turning it into what undoubtedly looked like a giant's checkerboard from the air.

After half an hour, we had only covered a fraction of the distance from one side of the lake to the other. We turned back, not wishing to undertake a ten mile round trip.

It goes without saying that we are very careful about venturing out onto the lake too early in the season. Every year, one or two careless snowmobilers or ice-fishing enthusiasts break through the ice at the GSL or Lake George (its nearby cousin), and end up fighting for their lives.

Often, when we're out cross-country skiing on the lake (yes, we do make use of the snowmobile trails for our own purposes), we'll see small groupings of people huddled by their ice shanties, fishing poles in hand, hoping to catch more than just a cold. Barbara's oldest son, Dan, an avid outdoorsman, always carries two screwdrivers with him when he is ice-fishing. That way, if the ice breaks through, he can use the screwdrivers like ice-axes to help pull himself out of what might otherwise become a watery tomb.

To be sure, most of the folks who ice-fish are exceedingly careful, and scrupulously avoid venturing out onto questionable ice if there is any doubt as to its integrity. My suspicion is that if you're tough enough to brave the winter weather to ice-fish, you probably have a pretty good idea as to what you're doing to begin with.

It's not just people, however, who end up being captured by the lake—sometimes objects do as well. My neighbor, for instance, waited too long before towing his shanty off of the lake. It now rests in Davy Jones's locker.

During the dead of winter, the GSL can be brutally cold. When the temperature drops into the single digits, and the wind starts whistling at 20 to 30 mph, the rapid movement of air across five miles of ice can produce a horrendous windchill factor. Psychologically, the coldness can feel even worse when you look up at the sky and see the sun, shining piteously near the horizon like a low watt light bulb.

Often, when the mood hits us, Barbara and I will use our camp as an outpost for North Country winter adventures. The only problem is the length of time it takes for the cottage to heat up once we arrive. Barbara's grandmother used to say, "A watched pot never boils." This maxim applies equally as well to a wood-burning stove. The fact is that not only the interior air, but every single object in the camp—the silverware, sheets, curtains, and so on—has to be raised to the same temperature; otherwise the camp stays cold.

To allow sufficient time, we generally head outdoors after lighting up the stove. Out on the lake, looking across miles of ice, the same realization hits us every time: this must be how the Sacandaga Valley once looked—minus the farms and towns—before it was forever turned into a mighty reservoir!

RING OF FIRE

THE *RING OF FIRE* TWICE YEARLY BRINGS UNITY AND COMMUNITY TO THE GREAT SACANDAGA LAKE

The Ring of Fire is a GSL tradition, celebrating the near-beginning of the lake season on the Fourth of July weekend, and its end on the Labor Day weekend; a symbolic return to more primitive times when humans huddled around campfires to ward off the cold and pesky hoards of insects. The tradition began around 1990, when a Mayfield resident named Agnes Gilbert, and her daughter, started encouraging other lake-side residents to celebrate the year by setting up bonfires on their beaches.

By good fortune, beach cleanup day was worked into this schedule, thereby allowing homeowners the opportunity to clear off debris from their properties, and to burn accumulations of bush and wood without reprisals from the authorities.

Now, when the Ring of Fire is celebrated on a clear night, the sight of hundreds of flickering bonfires surrounding the lake under a canopy of bright stars is simply breathtaking. At its height, the Ring of Fire is a feast for the senses; a night of sights and sounds as the ebony sky explodes into a dazzling array of fireworks and colors, and you sit listening to the whistling of launched rockets, sizzling sparklers, and the thunder of distant fireworks.

For two nights a year the Great Sacandaga Lake becomes a community united by a common ritual.

Aside from the esthetical considerations of joining together as a community, the Ring of Fire is a veritable bonanza for camp owners since it affords them the opportunity to purge their yards of downed tree limbs, branches, broken picnic tables, old boards, and just about anything else that may be combustible.

The fact that nearly anything can be burned was driven home to me just recently. One of my neighbors had an old boat that had been damaged beyond repair. When the night of the Ring of Fire arrived, he propped the vessel up on its end, garnished it with branches and timber, and set it afire. The boat lit up like a torch, shooting flames and sparks high into the night sky. I'm convinced that for that one evening there was no bonfire brighter on the lake!

To the two of us, it seems that the campfires just keep getting bigger and bigger from one season to the next. Some camp owners routinely set up huge sections of logs and timber, creating literally two-story-high bonfires. When one of these monstrosities gets going full blast, you don't want to be standing by too close or you'll get more than your eyelashes singed.

We live next to Diamond Point, where several shoals routinely emerge in mid-August, the most significant of these being Rock Island. Several holiday weekends ago, we looked out at the lake and saw not only the perimeter ablaze with bonfires, but Rock Island as well. Lo and behold, some imaginative soul had furtively rowed out to the island and set up a campfire, creating what then became a centerpiece for residents in the area of Diamond Point to enjoy.

No doubt, one of the most enthralling experiences of living on the Sac would be to boat out to its center during the Ring of Fire, although this could also prove to be a dangerous situation if everybody simultaneously came up with the same idea. Imagine the unreal sight of looking all around you and seeing the lake blazing with firelight—a complete 360-degree circle!!

The Ring of Fire is truly a night to remember.

Hikes

A CLUTE VIEW

THE VIEWS FROM CLUTE ARE CURT, BUT CUTE

There's an interesting rocky abutment, at an elevation of over 1,700 feet, that towers quite literally above North Shore Road as you drive northeast toward Conklingville: the cliffs on Clute Mountain. The mountain was named after a local pioneer named "Old Man Clute." The bluffs are visible roughly two miles south of Allen Road as you head east on County Route 4.

After the two of us stared up at the cliffs from the roadside, we knew instantly that this mountain would provide excellent views of the GSL, from a vantage point virtually opposite Shippee's Ledge on the South Shore Road—only with views much closer to the lake and without the interference of hills.

Choosing a stretch of land that was unoccupied by camps, we began bushwhacking up the mountain. For anyone doing this hike, be sure to get permission from the appropriate landowners before crossing private lands.

The climb up was steep and rugged. There were several huge bluffs that had to be negotiated, and always we were proceeding at an angle severe enough so that we would have tumbled for some distance had we lost our hand and foot holds.

Within a short time the humming of the cars on the highway below had receded into the distance, with our world turning from water and asphalt to rock and trees. On the way up, there were several ledges where you could catch fleeting glimpses of the lake.

"How are you doing?" I called down to Barbara, who was a short distance below me.

"Wishing I was a bird just about now," the answer wafted up.

I waited until Barbara caught up. "I think we're almost at the top," I announced confidently.

"What makes you so sure?"

"The broken bottles all around us," I replied with a sweep of my arm.

"Oh, great!" Barbara moaned. "What kind of people would bushwhack to the top of a rugged mountain, just so that they can throw bottles onto the rocks below?"

I must confess that I, too, was puzzled by this point. It's been our experience that if a hike is demanding, most of the partygoers and ya-hoo-ers lose heart and stay down by the roadside.

We climbed up the remaining escarpment and came up onto the top of the cliffs. . .

. . . Only to get the surprise of our lives!

There, right in front of us, was an old dirt road that led up to the overlook.

Frankly, I was flabbergasted. No wonder there were so many broken bottles lying around. Anybody with a four wheel drive vehicle (and permission from the landowner) could easily come right up the trail, with six-pack and all. The feeling was akin to the experience of climbing up Whiteface Mountain near Lake Placid, expecting peace and solitude, only to discover a fortress of rock, and the peak swarming with people.

Still, we felt exhilarated by our climb, and sat on the ledges quietly eating oranges and admiring the panoramic view. Although the view to the Conklingville Dam was blocked by hills, we were essentially able to look down to the northeast end of the lake. The hills facing us—Gray Hill, Cooks Hill, and Woodcock—were easy to distinguish, and we were able to follow the river for quite a distance as it meandered southwestward.

After lingering on top for a while, we were ready to start down, but this time taking the less demanding route via the jeep trail. After all, we were curious to see where the makeshift road came out onto North Shore Road. Just as we started down, we encountered two young men coming up with guitars slung over their shoulders.

We stopped to exchange pleasantries. Barbara mentioned that I also played guitar, classical and pop, and this lead us into a brief conversation on music. They liked Neil Young and the Grateful Dead. Generously, they invited me to jam with them, but I declined, for we had other places to visit that day.

I should mention that I was greatly impressed that two young men should make the effort to hike—not ride, mind you, but hike—up the mountain so that they could sing and play music at 1,700 feet. It gave Barbara and me a whole new understanding of the 'rock' in Rock & Roll.

The jeep road down was surprisingly steep. We arrived at the bottom within twenty minutes and, sure enough, came right out onto the North Shore Road some half mile or so further east than where we had started our bushwhack.

Every time I look up at Clute Mountain now, I think of those two young men sitting up on the ledges, strumming guitars, and singing Neil Young and Grateful Dead music.

MOOSE MOUNTAIN MADNESS

MOOSE MOUNTAIN IS NEAR WELLS, AND WELL WORTH THE BUSHWHACK FOR VIEWS OF PUMPKIN HOLLOW AND THE SACANDAGA RIVER

Moose Mountain has intrigued us for many years. Every time we drive north along Route 30, we see it filling up a good portion of the sky as we pass Pumpkin Hollow Road on the way to Wells. The shoulder of Moose Mountain comes right down to the Sacandaga Campground, which is located on the western side of Route 30, by the Sacandaga River.

What makes Moose Mountain so appealing are the huge cliffs that dominate the second summit on the mountain, quite visible from the road.

In October of '93 we decided to hike up to the cliffs, only to discover that hunting season had begun, and that the woods were teaming with riflemen. Exercising good judgment, we scurried back down in a jiffy.

The next time, we decided to do the hike in July. "No hunters now," Barbara stated with finality. "Remember. We're doing a bushwhack—not getting bushwhacked." Her eyes met mine. "Did you remember to bring your compass?"

"Absolutely," I replied. "In fact, I brought two along just in case we want a second opinion."

That was good.

You see, Moose Mountain doesn't have a trail. It's a bushwhack, meaning that you do the hike by using a compass and referring to landmarks, often with a trusty topo map in hand. It doesn't hurt to bring along a good dose of common sense, either.

The hike to the top of Moose Mountain is about one and a half miles long, with a gain in elevation of 860 feet or so. We started off from Route 30 about a quarter mile south of the Sacandaga Campground, at a large pulloff on the opposite side of the road that's pretty hard to miss.

Following a compass reading north/northeast, we headed through the woods, slowly gaining altitude. After two-thirds of a mile, we reached a series of bluffs, one after the other, and negotiated cliffs thirty or forty feet high in order to keep moving forward. After a mile, we had reached the top of some rocky ledges, mostly tree covered, and were able to get limited views to the south of the Sacandaga River and Route 30. On one section of the ledge, there was an enormous boulder that I climbed up onto for a better view of the valley.

From here, we proceeded in a northwesterly fashion, and finally arrived at the base of some high cliffs that didn't seem climbable at first. Barbara threw away her swisher (we both carried small leaf-covered branches to sweep away the black flies and biting insects that followed us like a cloud), and grabbed hold of available tree limbs and rocks in order to pull herself up. I followed suit. Up and up we went, following an incline that was steep and challenging. There was lots of talus below, and we knew that there would be additional heaps of rocks and two bruised hikers at the bottom if we weren't careful and started a landslide.

In about ten minutes, we had reached the top of the cliffs. We immediately came to a huge clearing, consisting of one formidable looking rounded ledge shaped like a giant's forehead that provided superlative views of the southern and western Adirondacks.

Cathead Mountain, which we had climbed four years previously, was clearly identifiable with its jutting fire tower. Two sections of the winding Sacandaga River were also quite recognizable. The other mountains, such as Finch Mountain and Mount Dunham, were not familiar to me other than names on the topo map.

We paused to eat lunch on this gloriously exposed ledge. Needless to say, there was a complete absence of other hikers. Undoubtedly, negotiating one and a half miles of trailless woods is a deterrent to any hiker those main enjoyment is following a well-defined trail and not having to worry about veering off course.

After twenty minutes, we started the climb back down, setting off on a south/southwest course once we had reached the precipice's bottom. This time, we steered a little to the north so that we would avoid having to climb up and down the series of hills and cliffs that had impeded our progress during the first half of the hike.

Near the last quarter mile of the journey, it was quite possible to proceed without compass just by using the distant sound of cars humming along on Route 30 as a directional. The experience reminded me of the time that a friend and I had emerged from Mitchell's Cave, by the Noses in Montgomery County, only to discover that darkness had descended while we were caving. Even with our helmet and flash lights blazing away we were not able to find our way out through a mile of woods because the feeble trail we had hiked in on was indistinguishable at night. Thoroughly soaked, we began to fret about what it would be like to spend the night in the woods. What saved the day for us was that we were able to hear the faint whirring sound of cars and trucks on the New York State Thruway, and that sound unerringly guided us down and out of the woods.

Fortunately, Barbara and I were hardly facing the same predicament here, and our first major attempt at a bushwhack of any significant length proved to be a roaring success. We burst out onto Route 30 only a hundred yards or so from where we were parked.

I felt a renewed appreciation for the magical powers of the compass, and to the fortuitous circumstances by which the Earth has magnetic poles. Clearly, without a compass for purposes of consultation, a hike of this nature would be considerably more intimidating, and quite a bit less certain.

SACANDAGA WATERFALLS

THE AREA AROUND THE GREAT SACANDAGA LAKE ISN'T ALL JUST VALLEY AND FLATNESS

When the Schoharie Reservoir in Schoharie County was created by the impoundment of Schoharie Creek at Gilboa Dam in 1926, two prominent waterfalls—Devesago Falls and Gilboa Falls—were obliterated in one fell swoop. Were there any waterfalls in the Sacandaga Valley that met a similar fate, literally drowned as the valley filled with water in 1930?

The answer, fortunately, happens to be no. A few small rapids and several dam-created cascades along the Sacandaga River may have come to an inglorious end, but otherwise the Sacandaga Valley has simply been too flat and featureless to produce any waterfalls that might have been endangered by the creation of a large reservoir. To be sure, several thousand years ago, when the last glaciers were retreating and a postglacial lake in the Sacandaga Valley formed, a small waterfall may have arisen at the lake's northeast end in Conklingville, where a containing wall was gradually worn down, ultimately causing all of the waters to escape until the lake was recreated in this century by engineers. But this was all.

If there are no waterfalls presently along the Sacandaga River, either at the inlet or outlet to the Great Sacandaga Lake, then does this mean that there are no waterfalls to be found at all in the valley?

If we confine ourselves to the floor of the Sacandaga Valley, then there is little to see but the lake itself and some minor rapids where the river enters and exits the lake. However, there are major hills on both sides of the valley extending upward, and along these we can encounter a fair number of prominent streams of varying sizes that flow into the Great Sacandaga Lake. The most notable of these are: Skinner Creek, Anthony Creek, Mayfield Creek, Jackson Creek, and Cranberry Creek (flowing down between Vail Mills and Northville into the lake's north shore); Beecher Creek, Sand Creek, Glasshouse Creek, Paul Creek, Allentown Creek, and Bell Brook (flowing into the north shore of the lake between Edenburg and Conklingville); Batcheller Creek, Deming Creek, Gordons Creek, and Daly Creek (flowing down between Batchellerville and Conklingville Dam into the lake's south shore); and Fayville Creek, Hans Creek, Frenchman Creek, Beaver Creek, and Kennyetto Creek (flowing into the south shore between Fayville and Broadalbin).

Assuming, rather optimistically, that one out of every five streams coming into the Sacandaga Valley contains a waterfall, how does one go about determining which of the streams are waterfall bearing?

To begin, driving around the 125 mile perimeter of the Great Sacandaga Lake to survey the streams as they enter the reservoir is not likely to prove helpful. The Sacandaga Valley is essentially gravel filled from the last glaciation; for this reason, as the creeks flow into the lake, they tumble over similar looking streambeds composed of loose rocks and stones—a poor foundation for waterfall formation. It is only by trekking up into the hills that the streambeds begin to reveal their true individuality, and become less uniform in character.

Neither are topo maps all that helpful. The tallest waterfall in the valley is no higher than twenty feet, a geographical feature not likely to be big enough to reveal itself on most topo maps. In the event that you come across a more detailed topographic map, look closely for compressed contour lines crossing over a blue stream line, which may reveal a waterfall's presence.

In the Sacandaga Valley, there are four waterfalls worthy of discussion. They are uniquely different from one another, both geologically as well as historically, with each one offering an interesting view of past life in the Sacandaga Valley. We are talking here about: Eggleston Falls, the falls on Glasshouse Creek, the falls on Beecher Creek, and the falls on Cranberry Creek.

Of these, the most famous by far is Eggleston Falls, located on Black Pond Creek, just above the stream's confluence with Daly Creek. The waterfall is likely named after Samuel Eggleston—an early settler in the Cornith area—or one of his descendants. The falls have also been known as "Hamilton Falls," the name of a former owner, and as "Three Pools," a name still used by many of the locals.

The falls consist of several ten to fifteen foot high cascades set into a picturesque gorge, with tumbles of rocks and carpets of pine needles beneath a canopy of tall pines. Although Eggleston Falls has always been privately owned, it was a favorite recreational site in the past. Several buildings, a pavilion, a rustic log footbridge spanning the creek, and wonderfully carved wooden pieces remain on the property, which is now being used for special occasions and events. Please take note that the falls are on posted land, and should only be visited if permission is obtained first.

Eggleston Falls can easily lay claim to being the most widely viewed and recognizable cascade in the entire Sacandaga Valley, but anonymously so. The falls appeared incognito in the movie *Billy Bathgate*, and provided the spectacular background for the scene where Nicole Kidman disrobes and jumps into a pool of clear mountain water below a tumbling waterfall.

Fly Pond, several miles to the west of Eggleston Falls off of Horse Hill Road, was also included in some of the shots.

The only other area in the Sacandaga Valley to be similarly captured on film in a nationally released full-length feature is the now defunct town of Osborn Bridge, long buried under the waters of the Great Sacandaga Lake, which was featured in the 1915 movie *Heart of Jennifer* staring Hazel Dawn.

Not too far from the falls is a huge boulder called *Tory Rock*, where legend has it that two Tories and an Indian were captured by Continental militia and brought to Fonda for interrogation. Such an incident suggests, then, that Eggleston Falls and the surrounding area have been known about by Native Americans for many centuries, and by colonists since at least the early 1700s.

The falls also remain inexorably linked with Ira Gray—a legendary Sacandaga woodsman and storyteller who lived next to Daly Creek, only a half mile or so downstream from the falls, and whose name was given to nearby Gray Hill.

The area around the falls is now being advertised as McArthur Park.

Proceeding directly west from Eggleston Falls, across to the opposite side of the lake, are a series of small falls on Glasshouse Creek—a tiny stream that rises in the northwest hills, and which flows into the Great Sacandaga Lake between West Day and Day Center.

Glasshouse Creek Falls consists of three modest plunges over ledges ranging from four to six feet in height, starting at a point just below the confluence of Glasshouse Creek and a tiny tributary. The area by the falls is characterized by huge jumbles of carved bedrock and giant boulders.

Along the north bank of the lowermost falls can be seen a long stone wall embankment—ruins from an earlier time when the falling waters were utilized for hydropower by a factory that apparently stood right over the stream. What's interesting about the site, and other similar places as well, is how quickly the erosive power of natural elements such as wind, water, and the action of life itself can virtually erase the presence of humanity in less than a century.

Just how did Glasshouse Creek acquire its name? According to Nancy Morris, Town Historian for Day, the factory that once stood over the creek was involved in glass making, much like the glass factory that previously stood southeast near Lake Desolation, but no one in the area remembers who owned the factory, or exactly what kind of glass products were produced.

Please take note that the falls are also on private property, and obtain permission before visiting the site.

Southwest of Glasshouse Creek, proceeding along the North Shore Road into an area known as Beechers Hollow, are the falls on Beecher Creek. Beecher Creek is a moderate sized stream that rises near Tenantville, and which flows into the Great Sacandaga Lake by the Edinburg Marina.

The falls are roughly twenty feet high, and cascade over huge ledges of dark shale. In late summer, one could almost walk straight up the towering ledges as though they were giant steps (although such derring-do is not recommended). During the springtime the water turns a frothy white, and becomes white as chalk against the shale's blackboard gray.

Just downstream from the falls spans the last remaining privately owned covered bridge in Saratoga County. The twenty-nine-foot-long Queen Post Truss bridge was built in 1879 by Arad Copeland so he could bring his cows to pasture on the opposite side of the creek. At that time, Copeland had a carriage factory in the white building, which still stands just upstream from the falls. This, of course, was in the days when the valley consisted of fields and forests—years before the Sacandaga Reservoir was created.

At the top of the falls, some several hundred feet further upstream, can be glimpsed the remains of an old dam that was once used for power generation. At one time there were six dams in close proximity. As a reflection of how times can change, over a century ago Beechers Hollow was a thriving river-based community, replete with numerous homes, a grist mill, a carriage factory, blacksmith shops, a tannery, a sawmill, a cider mill, a mop roller factory, and even a coffin maker—all dependent on the rushing waters of Beecher Creek. Now, none remain.

The top of the falls can be viewed from a parking area just uphill from the covered bridge. To reach the bottom of the falls, follow the well-manicured footpath down to Arad Copeland's bridge, then cross over the stream. The bridge is open to the public as the result of restoration work started in the fall of 2000 and just recently completed.

The fourth waterfall is located in a completely different section of the valley, overlooking the GSL at a point where it is broadest—over five miles across! From the hills looming above Northampton Beach and Sacandaga Park (a tiny village directly off of Route 30) descends Cranberry Creek, a stream that ultimately flows into the Great Sacandaga Lake at the village of Cranberry Creek—a small town whose fate was sealed when the valley was permanently flooded. Cranberry Creek got its name from the cranberry filled bog at Tamarack swamp through which the stream flows.

A small ravine is located at the end of Warner Hill Road, just downstream from the point where Warner Hill Road crosses over a small wooden bridge and becomes a jeep trail continuing uphill. Contained in this ravine, which is formed by a tiny tributary to Cranberry Creek, is a ten foot waterfall that comes alive in the early spring when torrents of water are gushing down from the nearby mountain tops. Take note that the waterfall is on private land and obtain permission if you plan to hike down to its base.

Just downstream from the base of the falls is the tiny stream's confluence with Cranberry Creek. It is also the point where an artificial pond was created many years ago so that the waters of Cranberry Creek could be temporarily held, with some diverted to Sacandaga Park and the rest left to continue downstream to power a variety of mills in and near the village of Cranberry Creek. A red utility shed standing in the middle of the pond reveals that the site is still being maintained and utilized.

What's more, this holding pond is merely part of a much larger system. If one were to follow the jeep road paralleling Cranberry Creek uphill for two-thirds of a mile, you would come to the Sacandaga Park Reservoir—a small artificially created mountain lake that collects the spring snowmelt, and then releases it slowly during the summer.

What was the original purpose for this mountain reservoir?

Years ago, a famous amusement park and resort area known as Sacandaga Park existed next to the Sacandaga River. With so many tourists and visitors gathering at Sacandaga Park during the summer months, the need arose for a dependable supply of clean drinking water. Ironically, the Sacandaga River, so close at hand, most likely proved to be an unreliable source of potable water due to upstream industrial pollution. As a result, the Sacandaga Park Reservoir and the lower containment area were created in 1898, along with a proper sewage system, so that pure water could be supplied steadily to the park.

The glorious days of Sacandaga Park ended with the creation of the GSL, but not so for the waterfall, which remains to this day at a safe elevation above the floor of the valley.

Although much of the Sacandaga Valley's resplendent past has faded into obscurity over the last century, these four pretty waterfalls remain, and will remain for centuries to come, as a connection to a past time when the valley was filled not with water but with farms, covered bridges, mills, factories, and interconnecting communities; a time when waterfalls and dams served as the principal source of hydropower for the area. Like any natural resource, they deserve to be treasured and preserved for future generations to enjoy.

For waterfall enthusiasts, there are a number of other cascades that can be seen and enjoyed in the general area of the Sacandaga Valley. Further north up the Sacandaga River, between Wells and Speculator, can be found Auger Falls, Austin Falls, and Christine Falls. West of Auger Falls, on the East Branch of the Sacandaga River, is Griffin Falls, located next to a vanished industrial town.

Northeast of Hope Falls (another town that disappeared virtually without a trace in the early 1900s) are several waterfalls on Tenant Creek.

Near Wells, on a tributary of the West Branch of the Sacandaga, is Jimmy Creek Falls. Further west along the West Branch of the Sacandaga River are several waterfalls in an area as rugged and wild as one could hope to find in the southern Adirondacks.

Finally, between Wells and Johnsburg along Route 8 are several small falls on tributaries of the East Branch of the Sacandaga River.

A THORNY PROBLEM

JOIN US AS WE SET OFF FOR THE CLIFFS ABOVE GIFFORD VALLEY

The two of us have long been hiking enthusiasts, and often utilize Barbara McMartin's *Discover the Adirondacks* series of books to guide us to interesting natural places. Since we live at the GSL, we are constantly searching for hikes in the general area. For this reason it was with much excitement and anticipation that we headed out from Northville to Gifford Valley to hike up to the cliffs overlooking the valley. We were particularly drawn to this hike by McMartin's description of the views from the cliffs as being the best of any of the hills surrounding the Great Sacandaga Lake's enormous perimeter. This was all that we needed to know to get us going.

Gifford Valley is named after a family of settlers—for the most part farmers—who occupied the valley around 1860.

The climb up to the Gifford Valley cliffs begins only a mile or so down Gifford Valley Road from its intersection with Route 30. The cliffs are clearly visible and loom, mesmerizingly, off in the distance about a mile or so as the crow flies.

There is a plethora of old, abandoned logging roads going in the general direction of the cliffs. What Barbara and I basically did was to jump from one road to the next, all the time trying to maintain a compass reading of approximately 330 degrees magnetic north.

In itself, forging ahead by use of a compass presented no unusual problems for us. What did begin posing a problem, however, were the prickers! As we continued on, heading up higher and higher, the density of pricker bushes kept increasing exponentially, until finally we were getting so scratched up that we threw in the towel and headed back. This was clearly no place for shorts and a T-shirt.

That was adventure number one. Adventure number two began somewhat later in the season when we returned, this time wearing long, heavy pants and slick, protective jackets that could not be easily penetrated or seized upon by the pricker bushes. In addition, I had brought along a sickle, and was prepared to whack away at the dense underbrush, just as I had seen it done numerous times in the old *Jungle Jim* movies.

Once again we encountered the inevitable entanglement of prickers that seemed to sprout from everywhere, particularly where the old logging roads once flourished. The only good thing that could be said about having the pricker bushes so close at hand was that we could readily reach out any time we were hungry and seize a few blackberries to eat. In a way it was almost like a contest: Barbara and Russell versus the prickers, with each trying to seize hold and take a bite out of the other!

Up and up we went, negotiating what McMartin had described as an easy bushwhack with a vertical rise of 900 feet. Finally we reached a point where the gradual ascent leveled out, and we looked across a huge open area, almost like a miniature valley, that contained towering thickets of prickers and ensnaring bushes. And there, on the other side, continued the hill where the main cliffs began. We were now, literally, only a stone's throw away from our destination, but would have to run the gauntlet to get there.

Barbara looked at me and I looked at her. This was not going to be easy! McMartin had said that the hike was a bushwhack, but never once had she mentioned that it would be strewn with the densest, thorniest underbrush imaginable.

In we started, with me in the lead whacking away at the bushes to open up a passageway. Foot by foot we traveled, with each step hard fought and won over the resisting bushes. It took us probably fifteen minutes to make it through no more than several hundred feet of thicket.

Finally, we broke through to the other side and continued up the steep hill, avoiding the face of the cliff as much as possible. Very shortly we reached the top—well, the top of the best viewing area—and strained our necks to catch even a glimpse of the lake. Much to our disappointment there was no place on the escarpment where we could see more than a snatch or two of the lake; the whole ridge was completely overgrown with trees and bushes. The wonderful view that McMartin had so longingly described in her book *Discover the Southern Adirondacks* was simply not there any longer.

Later that day we pulled out McMartin's book and took a closer look. The revised date of publication was 1974, practically nineteen years prior to our hike. In that length of time a lot of things can change and apparently had. Undoubtedly, when McMartin wrote up her book, the abandoned logging roads were just beginning to develop a rudimentary system of prickers and there was yet no impenetrable forest of prickers below the cliffs. Furthermore, the top of the cliffs were more likely than not bereft of the trees and bushes so abundantly present to greet us in 1992. This was all second generation growth before us...

...At least all of this was what we thought at the time! We later met Barbara McMartin at a workshop at the Trailhead Lodge in Benson and had a chance to talk with her about our hike, which she had read about after a friend brought it to her attention. According to McMartin, it's likely we reached the wrong part of the overlook, for she contends that the views are still there. A later hike up to the cliffs proved that she was right.

Despite the trials and tribulations described, Barbara and I would still recommend this hike to adventurous souls looking for something off the beaten (in this case, thorny) path. My only cautionary note would be to do the hike in midwinter; and there are several good reasons for doing so. First of all, if the snow is deep, many of the pricker bushes will be buried or low enough due to the buildup of snow to be easily brushed aside by the sweep of a foot. Secondly, and best of all, when you get to the top of the cliffs you will probably be able to get some excellent views of the lake through tree limbs that are bare and leafless, thanks to winter.

In conclusion, we will remind the reader that the title of this article is *A Thorny Problem*. The solution to the conundrum? Do the hike in winter.

POTASH MOUNTAIN

GATEKEEPER TO THE ADIRONDACKS

THE SOUTHERN ADIRONDACKS AT ITS BEST

One of the most breathtaking mountains in the southern Adirondacks also happens to be close at hand; and while it may be relatively meager in height, at 1,751 feet, when compared to its loftier and more publicized neighboring peak, Hadley Mountain, at 2,653 feet, it presents an unusual rocky face that both commands and beckons.

We are talking about Potash Mountain, located just north of the village of Lake Luzerne (which was named in 1808 after Chevalier de la Luzerne, a French diplomat who was appointed Minister to the United States). The mountain is pronounced "pot-ash," and is unforgettable for two distinctive reasons: It stands as a monadnock, solitary and isolated in contrast to the other nearby mountains, and it possesses an incredibly steep, rocky face that looks as if the top 800 feet of one of the High Peaks had been carried down, and dropped onto the floor of the valley.

Potash Mountain was originally called *Potash Kettle Mountain* by early settlers because it resembled an overturned kettle of the kind used in years bygone for making potash. Over centuries, the name was shortened to Potash Mountain, but the appellation "Kettle Mountain" no doubt would have been a better choice in recognition of the mountain's unique shape and appearance. The native American name for the mountain was *Se-non-go-wah*.

For those who are not familiar with the term, *potash* is a product that was commonly produced in the Adirondacks back in the 19th century. The substance is an impure form of potassium obtained from wood ashes. Early settlers would quickly scoop up the ashes from burned wood and dump them into vats of water, which were called *ash sheds*. Due to its solubility, lye was leached out of the diluted ashes, and the residue was boiled down into *black salts*. These black salts were then brought into the village *ashery*, where further refinement in a brick kiln, at high temperatures, produced *pearl ash*. It was the pearl ash that was ultimately used by local shops for making soap, dyeing clothes, and scouring sheared wool.

Because of its unforgettable appearance, Potash Mountain was utilized by both Indians and early settlers as a natural landmark. A famous Indian trail, starting from the eastern Mohawk Valley, at one time crossed over the Hudson River near Hadley and Luzerne, and then proceeded north past Potash Mountain, where Route 9N currently can be found on its way up to Lake George. For centuries, it was used as a main thoroughfare. As far as we know, however, no native Americans—Iroquois or Algonquin—settled in the area, although they frequently camped along many of the streams and lakes, leaving behind hundreds of artifacts along the shore of Lake Luzerne where the present Hadley-Luzerne Central School is now located. This Indian trail was also used by Sir William Johnson on his travels from Johnson Hall in Johnstown to the Canadian region, suggesting that it was well known and utilized by European settlers as well.

Potash Mountain may well represent the quintessential mountain for those who look for the ideal—a huge monodnack of rock that rises steeply into the sky; an object so massive and vertical that you can stand at the bottom and look nearly straight up at people moving about at the edge near its summit!

The view from the top of Potash Mountain is very rewarding, and reminiscent of Vroman's Nose located near Middleberg, another mountain which also has a near vertical drop into the valley below. The only drawback to Potash Mountain is that its principal views are to the south, which means that the Adirondack Mountains to the north are essentially blocked, as well as the Green Mountains to the east.

Nevertheless, there are sights to see, both near and far. To the west is Hadley Mountain, some eight miles distant. If you look carefully—here, binoculars would be of help—you can make out the fire tower on the top of its summit. Hadley Mountain is considered to be one of the nicest hikes in the southern Adirondacks, and has a trail going up to its summit.

To the northwest, and close at hand, is Thomas Mountain (1,941')—the highest peak in the Luzerne area—which, at one time, had two trails leading to its summit. Neither exists any longer, however, and the summit has long been overgrown with trees. To the southwest is Coman Mountain (1,242').

If you look very carefully southward, you will see a tiny portion of the Hudson River off in the distance in the vicinity of Luzerne; and if you study the topography closely enough, you may be able to deduce the path taken by the Hudson River as it flows to the west of Coman Mountain. Unfortunately, the river itself is not visible.

Looking further south beyond the village of Lake Luzerne you will easily see Mount Anthony, a respectable 1,637 feet in height, looming northwest of the village of Corinth. Around 1850, hematite iron ore was mined from the southeast slope of this mountain and transported to Luzerne, where the ore was smelted.

To the southeast, Bucktail Mountain (1,824') can be seen, as well as nearby Fourth Lake. Second Lake and Third Lake, which are also close by, are not visible, however. Neither are Forest Lake, Lake Allure, nor Lake Vanare, which are all artificially created, and located almost due east of Potash Mountain (although Lake Vanare can be viewed from some outcroppings on the eastern side of the mountain).

Somewhat surprisingly, Lake Luzerne can not be glimpsed despite its relatively large size and closeness, being blocked by Rockwell Hill, a 920-foot mountain named after either Jeremy Rockwell, who operated the first sawmill in Luzerne, or one of his descendants.

The road that you see extending off southward into the distance is Route 9N, and provides a convenient landmark for orienting yourself to where you are in relation to Lake Luzerne.

The hike up is not high enough to cause any major changes in foliation or temperature. However, caution should be used if you are attempting the climb in early winter or spring, since huge sheets of ice frequently form over the trail, making passage difficult if not actually dangerous.

The mountain has always been extremely rocky for as far back as anyone can remember, but even more so after 1980 when a fire swept over its summit. The bedrock near the top, like much of the Adirondacks, represents some of the oldest rocks on earth.

According to John Bennett—who was born at the foot of Potash Mountain in a tiny, now abandoned house which still stands just east of the power lines on Potash Road—attempts were made at one time to extract ore from Potash Mountain, but the efforts ultimately proved futile. All that remains of the mine, which can be found near the bottom of the western side of the mountain, is a slight penetration into the earth of no more than several feet.

Bennett, a descendant of Abenaki Indians, probably knows more about Potash Mountain than any person living or dead, having hiked to the summit hundreds of times and having photographed the peak from all angles during all seasons.

Potash Mountain is situated in an area that has been referred to by many historians as the "gateway to the Adirondacks." If Luzerne is to be considered the "gateway," then Potash Mountain is surely the "gatekeeper," for it stands impassively overlooking the valley; a silent sentinel guarding the northward passage now formed by Route 9N.

BALD BLUFF

AN INTERESTING BLUFF, WITH AN INTERESTING HISTORY

When the Great Sacandaga Lake came into existence, one part of the valley remained unchanged—the towering hills on both sides of the Sacandaga Valley between Vail Mills to the south and the Conklingville Dam to the northeast. These hills potentially provide natural overlooks of the GSL, but one might legitimately ask: Are there any spectacular views to be had?

In Barbara McMartin's *Discover the Adirondacks* guidebook, mention is made of two hikes; one up to a pretty overlook of the Great Sacandaga Lake at Shippee's Ledge, and another up to the cliffs overlooking Gifford Valley and the more distant GSL (see chapter titled *A Thorny Problem*). Neither of these hikes, however, afford stupendous panoramic or close-up views of the lake. The cliffs at Gifford Valley are northwest of Northville and, thus, beyond the main body of the Great Sacandaga Lake. Shippee's Ledge is much closer to the lake, but it oversees a relatively narrow portion of water southwest of the Conklingville Dam.

Both views tantalize, but neither fully satisfy.

There is a third overlook, however, that not only tantalizes, but satisfies as well. It overlooks the Sac closest to its broadest section, which is nearly five miles across, and is near enough to the water's edge so that you don't get the uncomfortable feeling that you are looking through the wrong end of a telescope.

We're talking here about the cliffs on Bald Bluff which, it should be noted, are on private land, and should only be accessed with permission from the landowner.

Bald Bluff is a fairly inconspicuous 1,800 foot high mountain formed on the eastern part of the Sacandaga Valley, just northeast of Fayville. Although the name Bald Bluff suggests a rocky, treeless peak, it is somewhat of a misnomer, for the top of the mountain as well as its lower part is completely forested. Undoubtedly the name arose, just as it did for hundreds of other peaks in the Adirondacks—Bald Mountain, Bald Peak, Bald Top, or Bald Bluff—because at one time it was stripped away of its trees, either by fire or from logging.

Bald Bluff was originally known as *Bald Top*, and even in pre-reservoir days it was intimately involved with the Sacandaga Valley. In 1814 Daniel Stewart and a crew of workmen began constructing a double barrel bridge in the nearby village of Fish House. The bridge was superbly built, with huge graceful arches, and lasted for 112 years until it was prematurely destroyed by the rising waters of the Great Sacandaga Lake. Although the bridge was primarily made of wood, stone was still needed for the foundation and abutments, and the rocks used happened to be quarried from nearby Bald Top.

Undoubtedly, some of the early settlers climbed up to the top of Bald Bluff for a view of the valley which, then, consisted of a conglomeration of marshes, farmlands, small towns, and wooded areas. When the GSL was created, however, the view changed from a valley overlook to a sweeping panorama of the lake.

One might wonder, however, how there can be views from the summit of Bald Bluff now if the top of the mountain is tree enclosed and has been for many decades, perhaps even for a century or two. By good fortune, and perhaps aided, in part, by some human intervention, a rocky cliff-like overlook exists some seventy-five feet below the top of the mountain. From these lower cliff ledges, there are excellent views to almost as far north as Edinburg, all the way south to Broadalbin.

Sand Island and Diamond Point are easily seen to the southwest, and Sinclair Point is virtually right across from the cliffs. To the south is a small body of water named Shew Pond. Like the Sacandaga Reservoir, it is artificially formed, created by the impoundment of Cloutler Creek.

From the ledges on Bald Bluff, the views are high enough so that boats and watercraft look like tiny water bugs as they dash across the water, leaving behind in their wake strands of glistening, crisscrossing webbing. It is views like this that add the *great* to the Great Sacandaga Lake.

Looking for the Perfect Waterfall

What is a "Perfect Waterfall" Anyhow?

The idea of looking for the perfect waterfall took shape after Barbara and I went to see *The Last of the Mohicans* in 1992. In one part of the movie, Hawkeye, Chingachgook, Uncas, Duncan, Cora, and Alice, pursued by a Huron War Party, were able to temporarily avoid capture by taking refuge in a shelter cave concealed behind a waterfall. Having read James Fenimore Cooper's book of the same title, I knew that the waterfall and cave were modeled after Glens Falls—a series of cascades formed on the Hudson River between Glens Falls (the city) and South Glens Falls—and the fissure cave at the base of the cascades, now known as Cooper's Cave.

Don't bother trying to take photos of Glens Falls, or climbing down to view Cooper's Cave, however. The falls have been heavily industrialized, and can only be glimpsed through a chain-linked fence from the Glens Falls Bridge; and Cooper's Cave has been closed to the public since a stairway that descended from the bridge was removed in 1959. (Take heart, though. Talks have resumed about reopening the cave to tourists in the future.)

To Barbara and me, it was the fictitious falls at Glens Falls, as described in Cooper's book and the movie, that represented the quintessential "perfect" waterfall—a cascade with a secret cave concealed behind its curtain of water.

But do such waterfalls exist in real life?

After some intensive academic research—consisting of consuming two bottles of Walnut Crest Chardonnay as we immersed ourselves in local books on caving and hiking destinations—we finally determined that the odds of finding a local waterfall overhanging a secret cave were about the same as winning the Publishers Clearinghouse Sweepstakes.

Still, not deterred by these meager odds, we kept looking (focusing on the general vicinity of the GSL), and eventually found, if not the perfect waterfall, at least what we considered to be the *semi-perfect* waterfall—a waterfall that possessed both a nifty cascade, and a shelter cave as well. The only problem, however, was that the cascade and cave were separated by a distance of over 100 feet.

The cascade that we came up with is Jimmy Creek Falls, formed a mile or so upstream from the creek's confluence with the West Branch of the Sacandaga River. Please understand that Jimmy Creek Falls, as waterfalls go, is hardly in the same league as Niagara Falls, so scale back your expectations accordingly and you won't be disappointed. The cascade stands roughly thirty feet high, which is a respectable height, and consists of sloping slabs of bedrock.

On the plus side, unlike Niagara Falls, Jimmy Creek Falls is never overrun with tourists. The shelter cave, while not large, is close to the falls and spacious enough to accommodate overnight guests; and, judging by the couple of rusted tin cans we found inside the cave, it probably has. What's particularly noteworthy about the shelter cave is that you can curl up on the rocks and watch the falls thundering away only a short distance from where you're resting. As we quickly discovered, it's almost impossible to sit in the glen without visions of long-gone Indians and early settlers rising up in the mist created by the falls.

To get there, take Route 30 north up to Wells, turn left onto Algonquin Drive by the dam forming Algonquin Lake, continue for three-quarters of a mile, and then turn left onto West River Road. After several miles, you will cross over Jimmy Creek. From here, head upstream on foot along the east bank of the stream until you come to the waterfall.

Hats off to Hadley

Hadley is hardly just any mountain

In 1980, Barbara McMartin published her classic guidebook, *50 Hikes in the Adirondacks*, and almost single-handedly transformed Hadley Mountain from an obscure, occasionally-hiked mountain, into the southern Adirondack's premier peak. And Hadley deserves the reputation it has earned, for it is a fabulous mountain, with a fire tower that takes you high above tree line for panoramic views of the Adirondacks, as well as distant views of the Helderbergs to the south.

According to Edward Gazda, in *Place Names in New York*, the town of Hadley was named after Hadley, Massachusetts. There are others who claim it was named after an early settler, long since forgotten. Regardless, the mountain was named due to its association with the town.

Formed as part of a chain of peaks running along the southeast corner of the Adirondacks, Hadley Mountain stands alone at the southern end.

For us, Hadley Mountain has had special meaning since the mid-1980s—for reasons that will become apparent in a moment.

For me, Hadley Mountain served as my introduction to mountain hiking at a time when I was still young (was it that long ago?) and naive beyond my years. Until Hadley Mountain, I had been holding onto several monumentally foolish notions about what mountains should be like. First of all, I assumed that if you stood at the base of a mountain, you could look directly up at it and see the summit—much like Vroomans Nose in Middleburgh. How quickly I was disabused of this notion! When I arrived at the trail-head for Hadley Mountain, there was no summit to view—nothing but densely packed woods. Were it not for the fact that the woods were inclined, and continuously rising upward as I moved ahead, I wouldn't even have known I was on the side of a mountain.

(Note: There is one mountain in the southern Adirondacks where you can actually view the summit from the bottom. See chapter on *Potash Mountain: Gatekeeper to the Adirondacks*.)

In the process of ascending Hadley Mountain, I also made another remarkable discovery—that some mountains have *false summits*. A false summit is encountered when you've labored to reach the top of the mountain, only to discover that it's not, and that the trail still continues upward, only now in a new and unexpected direction. Hadley Mountain's false summit is a long, flat ridge that I reached at 1.0 miles. Having never hiked a mountain before, I erroneously concluded that I must be at the summit simply because I had been hiking for what seemed like an inordinate length of time, and had gained a fair amount of elevation in the process. But where was the fire tower purported to be on top? I kept walking. Within five minutes, the trail suddenly pitched upward again, and the realization hit me like a ton of hiking books. I was not on top after all!

Equally as naive was my belief that trails going *up* mountains went *straight up*, following the shortest distance from point A to point B! Very quickly I came to realize that trails—providing they've been well planned and correctly designed—zig and zag their way up the mountain. This ensures that paths don't become heavily eroded, and provides a more gradual ascent for hikers, who might otherwise overextend themselves.

On my first hike up Hadley Mountain, I reached a summit that was shrouded in dense clouds. What a way to start off one's hiking career! There was nothing to look at except my own two feet and the ghostly outline of the fire tower. Before I could puzzle out what to do next, a huge storm came sweeping over the top of Hadley Mountain like a tidal wave. I quickly put on my poncho, and hurried down the mountain while peals of thunder boomed all around me, and bolts of lightning nipped at my heels.

Several years later, with Barbara now in my life, I headed back to Hadley, this time making sure that the day was sunny and storm-free.

All Barbara could say was "What kind of trail is this?" as we started up. She had noticed that the path was strangely wide, with huge slabs of exposed bedrock. "It looks more like a road to me," she added. And she was right—literally. In the early 1900s, a series of forest fires had done a considerable amount of damage to the Adirondacks. To avoid further mishaps, state officials constructed a chain of fire towers on perimeter peaks around the Adirondacks, starting in 1909, to serve as an early warning system. Mount Morris, in Franklin County, was the first tower to be erected. Hadley Mountain was also one of the peaks chosen, with a rough and tumble road constructed so that rangers could negotiate the mountain using a jeep. In this way, several weeks of supplies could be brought up to the small cabin that still stands today, not far below the fire tower.

To be sure, the road is no longer used as a road, and hasn't been for some time. Rangers stationed at the top now backpack in everything they need, and Hadley Mountain has returned to a more primitive and natural state.

The climb up was uneventful, and we reached the summit within ninety minutes. Sitting down on the rocky mantle, we were rewarded with clear views to the south, west, and east. Then, after a leisurely lunch of ham sandwiches and oranges, we ascended the fire tower and, by looking over the tops of the forest on the northern slope of the mountain, were able to see several of the High Peaks further north.

While on top of the fire tower, we met a ranger in his early twenties who was very helpful in answering questions, and who pointed out some of the major peaks around us. What I remember most about the conversation, however, was his statement that he would, on occasion, run down the mountain, reaching the bottom—some 1,550 feet below and two miles distant—in sixteen minutes. Even on flat ground, that's a respectable eight minute mile! In Europe they have a name for this kind of athleticism—*fell running*. I leave it to your imagination as to how this name came about.

I have heard talk that a cave exists at the top of the mountain off to the northwest, but we have never been able to locate it. My guess is that it is simply a tiny fissure in the escarpment ridge, and perhaps we have even walked by it on our explorations without taking notice.

As we climbed down from the fire tower, we glanced one last time at the wide serpentine river visible to the south in the distance. Although we didn't realize it at the time, we had just had our first glimpse of the Great Sacandaga Lake—an area that would acquire huge significance to us in the decades to come.

Climbing Cathead

Cathead Mountain is the perfect hike if you want to take the whole family out for an afternoon's adventure

Like Hadley Mountain (see *Hats Off to Hadley)*, Cathead is heavily visited, and has been a crowd pleaser for generation after generation.

Although topo maps show the mountain to be at the relatively low elevation of 2,423 feet, don't lose heart and think that Cathead is just another ascent into a dense forest of tall trees. While there are views from the bare summit, what makes the mountain so enticing is its fire tower, which allows you to climb further up above tree-line to enjoy superb views of the nearby foothills. To the southeast you can see the upper section of the Great Sacandaga Lake, and as far southeast as the Helderberg escarpment; to the north, you can see a variety of small hills, including Speculator, Finch, and Hamilton, and as far north as Snowy Mountain (which, at 3,899 feet, towers over the west shore of Indian Lake).

We have climbed up Cathead Mountain twice, and have found the experience rewarding on both occasions. Despite the climb's short 1.3 mile length, be prepared for a fairly rigorous ascent of over 1,100 feet. Fortunately, the distance is so short that, by the time the kids start to realize that they are tired and complain about the unrelenting steepness, the summit is at hand.

You will know that you are near the top of the mountain when you reach an old ranger's cabin, whose porch provides a handy place to sit and rest for a moment.

Another couple of minutes of climbing and you'll be at the summit, where a very impressive fire tower rises from the bedrock into the sky and clouds. Like all fire towers still surviving in the Adirondack Park, this one seems to have been built to withstand virtually everything that Mother Nature can throw at it, and that includes gale force winds. Still, you may still feel a mild sense of unease if you climb up the metal steps to the observation deck when high winds are blowing, and the guide wires are vibrating like plucked piano wires.

Cathead Mountain stands as the northwestern sentinel of the Great Sacandaga Lake— a scant seven miles from Northville as the crow flies.

RAISING KANE

RAISING KANE IS NOT ABOUT HOOTING, HOLLERING, AND RAISING CAIN, OR RAISING (SUGAR) CANE IN THE HOT FIELDS OF GEORGIA. RATHER, THE TITLE REFERS TO RAISING ONE'S SELF STEP BY STEP UP TO THE SUMMIT OF KANE MOUNTAIN—WHICH, AS MOUNTAINS GO, IS ABOUT AS FAR SOUTH AS YOU CAN GET AND STILL BE IN THE ADIRONDACKS

Kane Mountain is one of those climbs that would be an exercise in misery—all effort and no views—were it not for the fire tower that takes you above tree-line for excellent views of the southern Adirondacks, including nearby Pine Lake to the northeast, and West Canada Lake to the south.

The first time we climbed Kane Mountain was in 1992, and joining us was a married couple named Neil and Harriet, who had come up from New York City for a visit. Neil, I should point out, is a climbing enthusiast, and leads hiking excursions down in the Westchester area.

"I'm a climbing enthusiast too," I assured Neil as we arrived at the trail head for Kane Mountain.

"That's right," Barbara chimed in, not being able to resist a quick retort. "Just look at that patchwork of bruises on Russell's legs. Around here it's called the mark of Cain."

Bruises, apparently, are a badge of honor if you're part of the NYC hiking community, so Neil looked on with respect and appreciation. My bruises happen to be the result of doing too much bushwhacking in deep gorges while looking for waterfalls.

The hike up Kane Mountain, I should mention, is not a particularly demanding one. In fact, you could probably do it even if you were using a walker—or a cane (Ooops).

The hike is only 0.6 miles in length and, altogether, it took us less than thirty minutes to reach the summit.

"We won't get any views from here," Barbara commented as we crested the top of the mountain, "that is, unless we climb up the tower."

Directly in front of us was a forty-foot fire tower, gleaming in the sun.

I quietly waited for Harriet's response, knowing what it would be.

"No kane do," she said.

Okay. So much for predictability.

Harriet, you see, is a bit timid about heights—a condition known as acrophobia. What I can't figure out is how Harriet can ascend a mountain that rises 580 feet above the parking area, and not be bothered until she has to climb an additional, measly forty feet up the metal stairs of a sturdy, well-maintained fire tower.

Unperturbed, Barb, Neil, and I scampered up to the top of the tower for views of the surrounding area. The day was clear and the views unobstructed, particularly of the Mohawk Valley, and as far south as the Black Head Mountains (Black Head, Thomas Cole, and Black Dome).

There are two other trails that lead down from the summit, one going north to the campground at Pine Lake, and the other east to Green Lake and Green Lake Road, but we chose not to do a round trip, and returned the way we had come. In the years since then I remember reading about a pair of hikers who got lost on Kane Mountain, but I think you would have to work exceptionally hard at it if you wanted to lose your way.

When we arrived back at the car, I was all ready to do another hike, but Barb, Neil, and Harriet were determined that we should proceed expeditiously to a pub in Gloversville for the afternoon's libation.

I was about to protest, but then thought better of it. After all, there was no point in causing a fuss and creating a Kane Mutiny.

Places to Visit

ROCKWELL FALLS

THE ADIRONDACKS' PHOTO-PERFECT WATERFALL

Anyone who has driven across the Route 4 bridge connecting Hadley to Luzerne would have to be blind, or traveling through unrelenting fog, not to be awed by the tremendous views on both sides of the bridge. To the south, directly below, is a narrow gorge through which the Hudson River is squeezed, and then expanded again as the waters are joined by the Sacandaga River flowing in from the west. You can often see groups of rafters and tubers being disgorged from the Sacandaga River, as Class III rapids meet with the pensive waters of the Hudson at the confluence of the two rivers.

But the Hudson River's pensive waters are just an illusion!

If you look off from the bridge to the north, you will see Rockwell Falls—a small, but powerful waterfall where the waters of the Hudson River are pushed through a narrow, rocky drop.

Rockwell Falls is named after Jeremy Rockwell, who operated the first sawmill on the west side of the river by the falls. The Indians called the gorge *Boutakeese*; but early settlers renamed the cascade *Little Falls*, calling it "Little" in order to distinguish it from the *Big Falls* at Corinth. I find it fitting that the Indian name for Luzerne and Hadley was *Ti-sa-ran-do*, meaning "marriage of the waters," for the Hudson and Sacandaga Rivers do seem momentarily wedded as they join together just downstream from Rockwell Falls.

We have been through the towns of Hadley and Luzerne on many occasions, and have visited the falls numerous times. Although there is a path on the west bank that leads directly to Rockwell Falls, it is on private land, and permission is needed in order to access the falls.

On our last visit, due to a relatively dry summer, we were able to walk across huge slabs of stream bed right at the top of the falls. The thrashing waters below were so agitated that they literally looked carbonated as the stream flowed away from the waterfall.

Because Barbara and I have an interest in caving, we were fascinated by the plethora of potholes that had been worn into the bedrock by the river's ferocity during high water times. There were potholes of all sizes and shapes; some several feet in diameter and several feet deep. One particularly large pothole still had two huge rocks and an assortment of pebbles in it—tools that the river had temporarily discarded, but will surely employ again during the next period of high water in order to further scour the potholes.

We were saddened to see that some of the potholes also had beer cans in them; the unfortunate fallout of nature interfacing with civilization.

"Oh, no!" Barbara suddenly cried out. There were several fellows on the opposite side of the falls, and one of them had just dived headfirst into the frothy waters below. The others immediately followed suit.

I just shrugged my shoulders helplessly.

"Don't they realize what could happen if the water is too shallow, or they hit an underwater obstruction?" Barbara lamented. Barbara works for the State Health Department, you see, and is very involved with programs for brain injured people.

I also work in health care, and have seen my share of young men and women who are now para- or quadriplegics because they dove headfirst into unknown waters, collided with an unseen object, and snapped their necks.

"It's amazing that any of us make it through our younger years," I commented. "Caution generally comes with age, but that's only because you've lived long enough to have more to lose."

Needless to say, the young men who dove into the pool of water below Rockwell Falls survived their plunge without incident. Probably the water was plenty deep, and maybe they had even checked it out earlier before diving in headfirst. Maybe.

Just for precautionary measures, may I commend to you Barbara's diving maxim: In unknown waters always jump in feet first if you must go in without firsthand knowledge of what lies below. It's far better to end up with a broken leg than a broken neck.

We also observed some kayakers trying to approach the falls from below. It was fascinating to watch their progress. Through considerable effort on their part, they were able to make their way upstream towards the falls, but only to a certain point. Then, with their double-bladed paddles rotating like windmills, they would suddenly hit what looked like a force field, only to be repelled backwards the instant they slowed down their paddling. As far as we could tell, the kayakers appeared to be in no danger of getting too close to the falls and being pulled in under the rollers!

I later picked up a postcard of Rockwell Falls at a shop in town and left with a smile on my face.

THE ITALIAN GARDENS OF BROADALBIN

A THROWBACK TO THE RENAISSANCE DAYS OF THE SACANDAGA VALLEY

Inspiration for hikes and adventures can come from many sources, some unexpected. One delightful source has proven to be old postcards. In another chapter, I described how we learned about the existence of *High Rock*—an historic boulder in Sacandaga Park—after uncovering a 1906 postcard. By good fortune, we lucked out again, this time discovering a 1907 postcard captioned, *View in Italian Gardens, Broadalbin, NY.* It portrayed a fantastic flower and plant garden, ornamented with Roman pillars, groomed pathways across manicured lawns, a sundial, marble benches, and an unworldly terrain in the background.

I was intrigued. So was Barbara.

"Do you recall seeing any reference to the Italian Gardens of Broadalbin?" I asked.

"No." She hadn't, and neither had I.

I did a quick mental calculation. The postcard I was holding had to be almost one hundred years old, more than enough time for irreversible changes to have taken place.

I shook my head and stated, rather fatalistically "Chances are the gardens no longer exist. Probably buried under a row of condos during the last half century," I hastily added. "What do you think?"

"I think we should take a look," Barbara sensibly replied.

And so we did.

The problem, however, was where to look. If the gardens still existed, they were obviously no longer being touted as a tourist attraction, for there were no road signs to direct the curious. On the plus side, however, Broadalbin is not a large village. What's more, it's a village that has only been minimally modified by the creation of the Great Sacandaga Lake. In fact, I would wager that the rerouting of Route 29 probably had as profound an impact. Consequently, we were reasonably optimistic that the gardens had not turned into sunken gardens below the waters of the reservoir.

We drove around Broadalbin for a while, going up and down the main streets. After finding nothing, and not being sure that there was anything to find anyhow, we decided to try a more direct approach. As I have said many times over, the townspeople in the Sacandaga Valley are consistently friendly and helpful. We made several inquiries in Broadalbin and learned, much to our delight, that the Italian Gardens still existed, although not quite in their past state of glory and splendor.

Following some simple directions given to us, we drove down North Street, turned east onto Maple Street, and then took the second left onto Meadow Street. Meadow Street immediately bends at a right angle, turning west, until it intersects Thompson Street.

From Meadow Street's right angle bend to Thompson Street, can be found the Italian Gardens. The pillars and main structures still stand, as well as huge areas of gardens, but the pathways and many of the figurines are gone. However, one can not help but be struck by the fact that some considerable efforts are presently being made to preserve the gardens.

The Italian Gardens, it should be mentioned, are located on private property. The gardens are gated and posted, and can only be glimpsed by looking over the hedges paralleling Meadow Street. Still, it is not necessary to actually walk through the gardens in order to appreciate their beauty from afar.

Historically speaking, the Italian Gardens were designed by Katherine Husted—a wealthy Brooklyn society lady, who used Broadalbin for her summer home. Being both civic minded as well as philanthropic, Miss Husted donated all of her creations for public use.

These creations, in addition to the Italian Gardens, included a small but beautiful lake with two small pavilions, several swan boats propelled by bicycle pedals, a multitude of weeping willows, and finally, the famous *swinging bridge* that crossed over Kennyetto Creek near the lake.

After Miss Husted died in 1921, the gardens went through a series of alterations. First, Arthur Chalmers purchased the estate, and had the gardens redesigned. Then, in 1972, Mr. and Mrs. Victor Christopher, Jr. built a structure in the eastern corner of the gardens.

As a point of interest, at least some of the pillars found in the Italian Gardens were reputed to be at one time part of the original Broadalbin Train Depot. They were moved to the Italian Gardens after the main part of the train station was destroyed by fire.

As to the fate of the lake, which was known as Husted Lake, according to a 1905 map of Broadalbin, it is no longer a lake; at best it can be called a pond. Originally, Husted Lake was artificially created when workers built an eighty foot dam to divert the waters from the Kenyettto Creek to power a grist mill and saw mill. In 1917, the dam was destroyed by a battering of logs and high waters, and the lake shrunk in size, becoming a pond again. Although a wooden dam was subsequently built, it was short-lived, and the pond has remained basically in its present condition ever since.

It would be interesting, of course, to explore the area of Husted Lake to see if remnants remain from the past—perhaps a foundation or two from the rustic bridge that once spanned Kennyetto Creek from the Husted's property to Lake Husted; or traces of the one hundred foot-long *swinging bridge* that crossed above the dam until it was destroyed by ice in 1936. (Note: You don't have to wonder for too long. Coming up is the chapter on *Husted Lake*.)

Alas, there is only so much of the past that can be glimpsed. Broadalbin, fortunately, remains a village historically rich with some of its past treasures still visible.

THE SAGA OF HIGH ROCK

JUST ANOTHER ROCK? HARDLY. AT ONE TIME, HIGH ROCK WAS THE PREMIER NATURAL ATTRACTION OF SACANDAGA PARK

Some day, by chance, you may come across an old postcard of High Rock, a huge glacial boulder overlooking the Sacandaga Valley that was a highly popular commercial attraction until the mid-twentieth century.

If you're familiar at all with the Sacandaga Valley you may wonder why High Rock, so visible in old postcards and early photographs, is no longer a prominent geological feature and tourist destination. The saga of High Rock, alas, is one of fleeting fame and fading wonderment—the Sacandaga Valley's equivalent of a shooting star.

High Rock's geological origin dates back to the Wisconsin glaciation, when mile-high glaciers dominated northern New York State. These glaciers, like brobdingnagian bulldozers, planed the land, gouging out huge areas of earth and rock and transporting millions of tons of glacial till, consisting of gravel, soil, and rocks, over vast distances. High Rock was one of many huge chunks of rock that were moved by the glaciers; rocks that we today refer to as *glacial erratics*.

Some 8,000 to 10,000 years ago, the earth's climate began to warm sufficiently to cause the glaciers to retreat northward. In the Sacandaga Valley, the departing glacier left behind a huge mound of debris (or moraine) between Broadalbin and Gloversville. As a result, the Sacandaga River, now blocked from flowing south into the Mohawk River, backed up, and a postglacial lake formed whose perimeter very much coincided with today's Great Sacandaga Lake. High Rock was also left behind, about two-thirds of the way up on the side of a large, bare hill overlooking the newly created lake.

It was during this period of time that the forest, previously eradicated by the glaciers, returned to the area, and High Rock became eclipsed as thick woods of towering trees sprouted around it.

The postglacial Sacandaga Lake, however, only survived for a short time, geologically speaking. Water flowing over the containment wall at the lake's outlet in Conklingville gradually wore down the rock wall, causing the lake to empty out. Except for a marshy area called The Vly—from the Dutch word meaning "low, swampy ground"—the valley changed from a shallow but sizable lake into a relatively dry plain interlaced with streams.

Several millenniums passed, with High Rock resting high above an obscure river valley, virtually hidden from view by the forest surrounding it.

And then, humans began to enter the picture, with occasional bands of Native Americans traveling through the valley, generally following the course of the Sacandaga River. It was they, these earliest of visitors, who gave the land its present name *Sacandaga*, meaning "land of the waving grass." As far as High Rock goes, however, it is unlikely that these roving bands of Indians paid it much attention, or even noticed it at all.

Centuries continued to pass, and a smattering of trappers began making their way into the region. Still, High Rock remained an unappreciated glacial boulder.

Then, in the early 1800s, a number of small factories—lumber mills, tanneries, and gristmills—cropped up along the rivers and streams in the Sacandaga Valley, and a series of small communities and towns (Fish House, Cranberry Creek, Northville, Broadalbin, Batchellerville, Osborn Bridge, just to mention a few) formed around the factories. The industrial revolution had finally reached the southern Adirondacks.

In 1875, a particularly desirable area of the Sacandaga Valley next to the Sacandaga River developed as the Fonda, Johnstown & Gloversville Railroad expanded its service northward to the village of Northville. Very quickly, this section of the valley grew into Sacandaga Park, becoming a renowned resort and amusement park, called by many "the gem of the Adirondacks," with its own miniature train, roller skating rink, house of fun, shooting gallery, sports island, rustic theater, waterslide, roller coaster, burro rides, and numerous recreational opportunities. The clean, fresh Adirondack air, which Sacandaga Park provided in abundance, was touted as a cure for almost any ailment that travelers arrived with.

Some time also in the late 1800s, the area directly downhill from High Rock was cleared of trees and, perhaps for the first time since the retreat of the glaciers, the huge boulder once again had a commanding view of the valley below. From High Rock, now devoid of trees, a visitor to the area could stand and literally take in a full panoramic view of the southern end of the Sacandaga Valley.

Undoubtedly, High Rock was named at this time as a result of two prominent features which defined the boulder—the fact that it loomed *high* above the valley, and that it was a very large *rock*.

As Sacandaga Park grew and flourished, High Rock also became an attraction in its own right, providing visitors a unique opportunity to escape the claustrophobic confines of the valley in order to see "the big picture," and the wide expanse of the Sacandaga Valley from above.

In 1901, James Hull of Gloversville built the High Rock Lodge—a modest size mountain house that was constructed a short distance uphill from the boulder. The lodge was accessible by a carriage road that started up from where current Route 30 parallels the lake, passing a hundred feet below High Rock, and then winding its way up and above the boulder to a point further uphill where the hotel was situated. Along the way, a series of cottages, or bungalows, provided lodging to tourists who wanted either to be closer to the rock, or desired accommodations separate from the main hotel.

In time, additional carriage roads and pathways were constructed, making all 300 acres of land accessible, and tennis courts, a softball field, flower gardens, and riding stables were added as well. Soon, the hotel was prospering as business boomed, and the mountain house quickly doubled in size in order to satisfy the increasing number of tourists seeking accommodations.

The High Rock Hotel went through a series of owners including, early on, Mr. Buckingham, who was known as "Old Buck," Ashley and Mildred Dawes, and much later, Tony Farrell.

"Bud" Darling and his sister, Grace Louckes, lifetime residents of the Sacandaga Valley, have the distinction of having been born at High Rock when their parents were employed at the lodge as caretakers. During those years, their father built a tiny subterranean stone cave right along present High Rock Road where a water pump was housed. The stone casement still stands, and even now can be entered for several feet.

A marvelous stone stairway with lighted posts went up to High Rock, and the stairs still remain, although heavily overgrown with moss and dirt. Up by the rock, a fancy pavilion at one time provided accommodations for weary tourists to sit and cool off as they made their way between the lodge and Sacandaga Park.

Although a separate entity in its own right, High Rock was nevertheless symbiotically and economically bound to Sacandaga Park. After all, it was Sacandaga Park that was the principal tourist attraction and main drawing card possessing, it should be noted, three large hotels—Adirondack Inn, The Pines, and Old Orchard Inn—to High Rock's one. At best, High Rock was a peripheral drawing card; a one horse show, in a manner of speaking.

Still, both places prospered, with the exception of an occasional setback caused by fire, and probably would have continued to do so if not for one significant happening that changed the character of the valley forever...

...In the mid 1920s, a decision was made by New York State legislators to flood the valley and create a huge reservoir.

Not surprisingly, the creation of the Sacandaga Reservoir had absolutely no *direct* impact on High Rock. The boulder and its surrounding estate were simply too high above the valley floor to be threatened by the rising lake waters.

But Sacandaga Park itself, "the Coney Island of the East," was doomed as soon as the decision was made to flood the valley. Most of the amusement park and buildings rested on the floor of the valley, not far from the edge of the Sacandaga River. As a result, when the wild waters of the Sacandaga River were intercepted by a newly created dam at Conklingville, two-thirds of Sacandaga Park vanished under water as the lake rose, and the glorious days of Sacandaga Park ended forever. Today, all that remains of the park's former renown are a smattering of cottages, a restaurant, golf course, and the old FJ&G train station, which until recently was used as an artist's studio.

The creation of the GSL also undermined the transportation system that brought tourists directly to Sacandaga Park. One year before the Conklingville Dam and valley preparations were completed, the Hudson River Regulating District Board notified the FJ&G Railroad that they had until March of 1930 to remove their tracks from 150 acres of land, and seven miles of right of way that had been condemned.

The railroad was also awarded $1,750,000 in damages to compensate for the loss of their Northville line. When March of 1930 arrived, however, railroad workers were still out in the valley frantically trying to take out track when the rising waters forced them to retreat to higher ground. For whatever reasons, the FJ&G Railroad had waited too long, leaving sections of track behind that can still be glimpsed underwater today by scuba divers.

The FJ&G Railroad ultimately chose not to reestablish the north line despite the financial settlement, and all tracks remaining above Broadalbin Junction were abandoned. Without the railroad, Sacandaga Park could no longer bring in tourists efficiently in large numbers, and business suffered as a result.

Even if the train line had not been lost, however, High Rock (and Sacandaga Park) might have faced an uncertain financial future. In the 1930s, Americans were already beginning to form a love relationship with their automobiles, forsaking mass transit systems such as trains, for the freedom and versatility that automobiles provided. As a result, loyal tourists who previously had come to High Rock every summer began to consider other vacation options; places that had not been accessible during the heyday of mass transit.

Even though High Rock was *directly* spared when the Great Sacandaga Lake was created, the *indirect* impact was devastating due to the huge boulder's close association with, and dependency on, Sacandaga Park; not to mention the loss of the FJ&G Railroad's north line, and the emergence of the automobile that allowed tourists to go wherever they chose. Visitors waned, and High Rock became unable to generate enough business to survive as a solo attraction. The business was sold to Reuben D. Buckingham in 1927, and then to Ashley Dawes in 1940. Later, attempts were made to run the bungalow, formerly lived in by Ashley and Mildred Dawes, as a restaurant. However, slowly but surely, High Rock Lodge fell into decline, and the forest began to creep back in, reclaiming the grounds in stages; finally, in 1951, the restaurant itself was destroyed by fire.

Only faint traces of a number of the cottages—a few stones from the old foundation, segments of plumbing, and a tiny stairway—remain, and these are slowly being subsumed by the earth. In 1956, the property was sold to Anthony B. Farrell. William LeLia is the present owner.

And the High Rock Hotel? Near where it once stood, a private home has been built, eradicating all traces of the hotel's past.

As for High Rock, the once famous glacial boulder of Sacandaga Park? It slowly faded back into obscurity as the forest grew up around it and reclaimed it once again.

High Rock is now on posted land, but there is no reason to visit it anyway. There is nothing to see anymore except for a large, undistinguished boulder surrounded by dense forest. High Rock is gone…

…for the moment, at least!

TENANT CREEK FALLS AND THE HIGH-DIVING DOG

THE TRUE STORY OF A DOG THAT PLUNGED OVER THE TOP OF TENANT CREEK FALLS

The hike in to Tenant Creek Falls is a popular one, and known to many residents and visitors of the Northville and Wells area. Our introduction to Tenant Creek Falls occurred in July of '93 when we decided to balance off some mountain climbs with a waterfall hike.

We didn't have any trouble finding Tenant Creek Falls, for we always carry a *New York State Atlas & Gazetteer*, which is basically a collection of large-scale topo maps. On the day of our hike we were by no means the only ones proceeding onto the trail. The trail-head parking lot was overflowing with cars; some undoubtedly belonging to fishermen looking to make a catch of the day, or to a few hardy souls making the trek up to Wilcox Lake and back. The rest belonged to hikers who were in various stages of arriving at or leaving the falls.

When the two of us reached the waterfall—which stands some forty feet high in a series of steep cascades—some young people had just finished swimming in the pool beneath the falls and were drying off. We later took a quick dip ourselves, and let me tell you, if it's cold water you like, then this is the place to find it on a hot summer's afternoon.

While Barbara sat below contemplating the falls, I scampered up to the top and, at some distance from the brink, crossed over to the other side. Within several minutes I was back down again at the base of the falls.

It's funny how little things come back to you at the strangest times, but as I was exploring the falls, an old limerick about a man and a fall kept going through my mind:

> There was a young fellow named Hall
> Who fell in the spring in the fall.
> 'Twould have been a sad thing
> If he died in the spring,
> But he didn't; he died in the fall.

I mention this poem because it does have some bearing upon what subsequently happened while we were at the falls. To put it simply, waterfalls, as beautiful and sublime as they may be, can be dangerous nevertheless if you're caught unaware. T-Lake Falls, for instance, which is located near Piseco Lake, has claimed the lives of a number of hikers and a variety of animals over the last several decades. The reason is that T-Lake Falls, like Tenant Creek Falls, has a rounded, smooth bedrock that slopes gradually down towards the edge of the falls.

The unwary, then, are slowly led to the edge, where they suddenly find themselves beginning to slide, unable to reclaim traction. Since the rocks are smooth and there are no hand holds to be found, hikers are swept over the edge to their doom, caught on a one-way trip like insects into a Venus Fly Trap.

Now, Tenant Creek Falls is fortunately no T-Lake Falls, whose height consists of a series of cascades and plunges with a total vertical height of 350 feet. Still, Tenant Creek Falls can be a force to be reckoned with, as Barbara and I found out that day.

Soon after we arrived, a party consisting of two couples and a high-spirited black poodle came bounding in, and settled down near us at the base of the falls. We said hello, and then entered into a debate with the younger man as to whether the cascade was called Tenant Creek Falls or Hope Falls.

Meanwhile, the older man, who impressed me as a sixty-five year old Rambo, started up the rocky slope with the black poodle, unleashed and dashing around beside him. When they got to the top of the falls, the poodle ventured out towards the top of the stream bed, presumably for a closer look. I guess dogs are a lot like people in this respect.

Barbara was about to say something about keeping the dog away from the top when it suddenly happened: on the rounded, slippery bedrock, the dog all at once began to lose traction, and started sliding down the slope.

As its speed began to increase, the poodle started making a beeline sideways as fast as it could to the safety of the drier rocks. For a second I thought the pooch was going to make it, for it seemed to regain its footing momentarily.

But that was only an illusion. Inexorably, the dog began moving forward again, picking up speed, and started the downward plunge over the sloping rocks. Somehow during its plunge, the dog managed to stay up on all fours, so that it rode the cascade down as if on a waterslide, albeit a potentially deadly one. Near the bottom, the poodle went over a ledge, and tumbled five or six feet into the pool of water at the base of the falls.

The dog, obviously stunned, now started swimming towards the rocky shoreline, but seemed in a daze, and unable to exit the water on its own power. The whole incident, up to this point, had probably occurred in the span of no more than ten seconds, and I was already ruing the fact that I didn't have my camera in hand to snap a prize-winning photo of the descent.

Because the other members of the party were between us and the falls, and were quite capable of rendering assistance, I didn't jump into the water to rescue the dog, but watched as the older lady waded in and, with the help of the younger woman poised on the rocks, hoisted the dog onto dry land.

Barbara was concerned that the dog might be injured, but as far as I could tell, it was merely stunned. The poodle stood around for a few minutes, very subdued and obviously shaken up, but then began to regain its bearing. Within five minutes it looked no worse for its experience.

For a human being, however, the ride down the cascade might not have been accomplished with such a favorable outcome. Dogs have four legs to maintain balance, and to keep from falling down and being banged around on the cascades. Humans, possessing two shaky legs, do not have quite the same advantage. In my opinion, if it was a person who had gone over the edge that day, we would have had to carry him or her out of the woods.

My advice to the unwary, hence, is to always keep dogs leashed around areas that can be treacherous—for the dog's sake as well as your own, since you might end up getting hurt while trying to affect a rescue.

As for us, we will always remember the day we saw the High-Diving Dog go over Tenant Creek Falls.

TORY ROCK

IF YOU LIKE GLACIAL ERRACTICS, THEN THIS IS THE ROCK TO SEE—A MONSTER OF STONE WITH A HISTORY

Near the confluence of Daly Creek and Black Pond Creek, just a quarter of a mile from Davingnon Road, is a huge boulder (a glacial erratic) known as Tory Rock. Egg-shaped and well over eighteen feet high, the boulder has walls that are so steep it is virtually impossible to scale them without a ladder or tree to prop up against.

Truly, there is nothing else like it in the valley!

It is for this very reason that the rock has a history that goes back almost 300 years, replete with several stories which reveal how it came to be named. Back in the 1700s, there was no Great Sacandaga Lake—only the Sacandaga River and its tributaries. Landmarks were scarce at that time and, when found, became important designations by which early trappers, Indians, frontiersmen, and militia navigated the impenetrable wilderness. Tory Rock, because of its large size and imposing presence, proved to be an outstanding landmark.

One of the old tales, centering on the boulder, goes back to the Revolutionary War, and can be found in John E. Boos's book *The Sacandaga Valley*. A group of British soldiers and Tories were camped out by Daly Creek near Tory Rock. History has it that they were discovered by a group of Continental soldiers who had camped out nearby. What followed was a battle in which the British were resoundingly defeated. No mention is made as to what happened to the Tories, but they probably met the same fate as the British redcoats.

Another tale has it that the giant rock was a meeting place for Tory spies. At these meetings, information was exchanged and vital secrets then carried northward. In one incident, the Continentals learned that two Tories and one Indian were camped at the rock. The next morning the Continentals swept down on the camped party, capturing them without a great deal of fuss. The Tories and Indian were then brought to Fonda, and that is as far as the historical record goes.

But from these encounters the boulder came to be known as Tory Rock.

The rock was well known to Ira Gray—also known as "Adirondack Ike"—who is probably the most famous woodsman to come out of the Sacandaga Valley. Gray lived near Brooks Bay on West Mountain Road, only a mile away from Tory Rock, and would often pass the rock on his forages into the woods, either while traveling alone or guiding a party. Gray, incidentally, died in 1982 at the ripe old age of ninety-five!

Tory Rock was also familiar to Mortimer Cook, who built a sawmill at Huntoon's Riffs, near the confluence of Daly Creek and the Sacandaga River. In fact, at one time there were no less than nine sawmills along the course of Daly Creek (which was spelled Dailey Creek at that time).

In the book *In Days Past*, by Nancy J. Morris (Town Historian of Day), mention is made that a famous "Old Indian Trail" once paralleled Daly Creek, and passed right by Tory Rock. The trail was frequently used by Indians, particularly raiding parties during the French and Indian War.

Tory Rock isn't the only geological feature in the area known by the preface *Tory*. If you have been to the Lower Bear Trail at Indian Ladder in Thacher Park, you may have passed by Tory Cave, a notable karst spring, where Jacob Salsbury, a spy, took refuge in 1777.

But back to the Sacandaga's Tory Rock. Boos describes the boulder as "about 18 feet high, slightly rounded on top" with "six sides, at not much of an angle" and with each side being "about 20 feet wide..." It is a monster rock, and Barbara and I have been to it on three different occasions. The last time we visited the boulder I pulled myself up part of the way so that I could look across the top of the rock, only to notice a beer can sitting squarely on top. I guess civilization had arrived at last!

(Tory Rock is undoubtedly on private land, even though it is not currently posted.)

WALKING THROUGH BOOT HILL

YOU NEVER KNOW WHAT YOU MAY FIND WHEN YOU WALK THROUGH OLD CEMETERIES IN THE SACANDAGA VALLEY

There are a number of cemeteries literally overlooking the Great Sacandaga Lake, which is not surprising considering that 3,872 graves from twenty-two cemeteries, including the ones at Osborn Bridge, Denton's Corner, and Day Center Flats, had to be moved from the floor of the valley to higher ground in order for the lands to be flooded.

Since cemeteries are frequently built on high ground to begin with, many of the outlying cemeteries were not affected when the valley was flooded, because of their elevated positions.

The two of us live near Fish House and, without sounding unduly morbid, have spent parts of several afternoons leisurely perusing the Fish House cemeteries at Shews Hill near the Methodist Church, named after Godfrey Shew (the areas first white settler), and at the old Presbyterian Church on Fish House Road, whose building has not been used as a church since 1919.

The cemetery on Shews Hill is peaceful and strikingly picturesque, and overlooks a quiet span of the Great Sacandaga Lake. Strolling through the grounds, we have noted such historic names as the Shews, Martins, and Sleezers. They, along with Alexander St. John, Isabel Parks, John Fay, Zebulan Algers, John Roosevelt, John Eikler, and Nicholas Lewis, were among the first settlers in Fish House.

Halfheartedly, I had hoped that several of the tombstones might have witty or funny verses on them—you know, in the vein of "Here lies 'til Gabriel's trumpet peals the bones of Shelby Sharp, who died while holding a steering wheel and woke up holding a harp,"—but I saw nothing except the serious and ponderous epitaphs that one typically sees on gravestones.

Although we were impressed at how nicely the grounds were maintained at Shews Hill, we were justifiably startled to see that the rows of tombstones continued right up to a building owned by the adjacent property owner. In fact, we noticed that a hinged door on this structure was being propped up by a pole resting on one of the tombstones. Talk about the dead aiding the living!

The cemetery on Fish House Road adjacent to the old Presbyterian Church, however, was a different story entirely. By contrast, this graveyard looked downright spooky and foreboding. Picture, if you will, ancient tombstones leaning in all different directions, and sprouting out of knee high grass. Then picture an old disintegrating church—so neglected, in fact, that tall trees have grown up in front of the building, obscuring it from the road—on one side of the cemetery, and what looks every bit like a haunted house, with peeling, white paint, on the other side.

"Someone should use this graveyard for the next *Blair Witch Project*," Barbara whispered to me as we made our way to the road. It felt good to be back in the sunlight and open space after being in this lugubrious cemetery. (Note: By the following year, the Presbyterian Church Cemetery had been properly tended to.)

Barbara and I ended our cemetery tour with a quick drive up to the Edinburg Cemetery on Route 4, between Edinburg and Northville. Earlier we had learned that Edward Sargent, the architect of the Sacandaga Reservoir, is buried there. We found his tombstone without much difficulty, located in the northeast corner of the cemetery.

The tombstone read: "Edward Haynes Sargent (1885-1954). Major A. E. F. 116th Engineers. Designer and Chief Engineer, Sacandaga Reservoir." To the left of the inscription was an outline of the Great Sacandaga Lake.

At the foot of Sargent's tombstone were three smaller markers: one for his wife, one for his son, and one, I presume, for his daughter.

It felt proper to end our graveyard jaunt by paying homage to Sargent, for we had truly come full circle from the prereservoir days to the days of the Great Sacandaga Lake.

If you are interested in knowing more about cemeteries in the area of the GSL, John E. Boos's book, *The Sacandaga Valley*, makes for informative reading.

SAND ISLAND MAGIC

IT'S ALWAYS PARTY TIME ON SAND ISLAND!

If you hear the distant cry of "It's party time!" you can bet that a boatload of revelers is heading out to Sand Island—the Great Sacandaga Lake's premier natural attraction for sand, surf, and sun-worshippers (in fact, lots of sun-worshippers).

What makes Sand Island so popular is . . . well. . . its *sand*. Sand Island is literally one huge sand box of glacial till that was left behind by the last retreating Ice Age, with beaches virtually extending around the full perimeter of the island. What's more, as the water level decreases during summer, the surface area of Sand Island grows dramatically to over 2–3 times its original size, which translates into more beach front, although less people, since by this time the season is well into late fall, and the water, not to mention the air, has turned colder.

The main part of the island contains its fair share of trees, which makes it an interesting area for casual exploration, or a leisurely walk. Like all of the islands, the trees on Sand Island consist of a second generation forest, thanks to the cutters who swept through the valley prior to it being flooded.

Sand Island is located near the eastern perimeter of the lake, north of North Broadalbin, and west of Benedict Bay. It is not hard to find. And if you happen to be walking around the island in the late fall, when the lake water level has dropped precipitously, and notice vague outlines of foundations, don't be surprised. Several houses and farms existed in this area prior to it becoming Sand Island.

If you look at an old topo map of the Sacandaga Valley—and we are talking pre-1930 here—you will notice that a road from North Broadalbin headed directly north towards present day Sand Island, and then continued on, bending eastward, to the village of Fish House, which was then called Northampton. At Sand Island, a second road headed off west, crossed over the Kennyetto Creek, and continued southwest to Munsonville. Several black dots can be seen along the roads, signifying homes that once existed.

Even before the Great Sacandaga Lake was created, the area by Sand Island was no stranger to water. Several major creeks flowed around the hill, including Frenchman Creek, Hans Creek, and Kennyetto Creek. And in the midst of all of this, to the north, west, and south, was The Vly, a vast area of marshy land that was a veritable sportsman's paradise.

When the valley flooded, all of these geographical points of interest disappeared. Indeed, Sand Island would have vanished too if not for the fact that it was slightly higher than the final level the lake water attained. Rock Island and Stump Island, two shoals that rise annually from the depths northeast of Sand Island, were not as fortunate.

Sand Island is shaped like the letter "E" when the lake is at full volume. When the island becomes fully exposed, as the lake level reaches its maximum discharge of water, it becomes shaped like a huge amoeba, with one protruding arm almost reaching down to the North Broadalbin Loop.

None of this background information matters much, I suppose, when you're headed to Sand Island on a jet ski or power boat with a six pack in tow. Still, it is worth noting, with some degree of awe, that you will be soon walking around on what was at one time the floor of the valley.

Sand Island has become so popular that, at times, it is literally ringed by concentric circles of parked jet skis, motorboats, party barges, sailboats, and what not. It is a wonderful place to go to if you like to be with people of like-thinking. On the other hand, it is not a wonderful place to go to if you enjoy being a hermit.

ADVENTURES

Buoys of Summer

Catching Waves on the Sacandaga River

River runners in the early twenty-first century have a dizzying array of choices for pursuing paddle sports, from kayaks shaped like bananas, to canoes built of space-age materials. Faced with all this glittering gear, Barbara and I prefer a low-tech route, selecting a time-honored, simple craft made of black rubber. When the summer heat turns oppressive, the two of us grab our inner tubes and head to Hadley and Lake Luzerne, where the Sacandaga River merges with the Hudson River.

The lower Sacandaga consists of a three-mile stretch of Class II and III white water between Stewarts Dam and Hadley, and drops sixty-six feet during its descent to create a paddler's paradise. It can also be a very crowded one: there are several rafting outfitters who take paying customers down the river, which adds to the traffic on the waterway.

Trust me on this. White-water tubing is every bit as exciting as white-water rafting. The inner tube provides an intimacy with the river that the flashy, self-bailing rafts can not possibly furnish, congested as they are with passengers. Barbara and I have drifted the Sacandaga many times, and will probably continue doing so until our skin becomes shriveled from old age—not from immersion!

But first, a few basics. Years ago, most tubers wore bathing suits and sneakers, period. This is no longer sufficient. You are now required to wear a U.S. Coast Guard-approved personal flotation device. You'll be safer, you'll feel safer, and your upper body will stay warmer on a chilly day.

Headgear is also strongly recommended. When tragic accidents occur, they have generally happened because someone has been thrown from their craft into the water and knocked unconscious. While the Sacandaga is relatively tame compared to the raging Hudson River Gorge, take note that during your trip you'll be passing over and around some very big rocks. Many of them are only inches below the water's surface; it's their proximity to the top that generates the waves. Wearing a kayaker's helmet may help avert disaster.

Don't drink alcoholic beverages while tubing. Far too many water-related accidents occur because people have been drinking and lost both their coordination and good judgment.

Which leads to another important point. Be sure to bring along a friend or two. There's safety in numbers, particularly if the unexpected happens and turns ominous.

We use a large tube, about four feet in diameter, that may have begun its working career on a big dump truck or tractor. On the Sacandaga, Barbara and I have seen some tubes with wooden platforms attached to their undersides so that the tuber is protected from rocks passing beneath. Although my rear end has bumped against many rocks while dangling through my inner tube, I have never been particularly bothered by the impacts. Almost without exception, all of the rocks you're likely to encounter are smooth thanks to the wearing action of the water. Still, a tube with a bottom affixed does provide one more level of protection, and probably even adds a little ballast to help keep the tube from flipping while running big waves. By the way, I've never had, nor seen, an inner tube blowout on a river trip; leaks that develop tend to be so slow they can be repaired after the ride is over.

Another consideration. If the water is cold and the day not particularly sunny or warm, you might wish to wear a quarter-inch thick neoprene wet suit, the kind favored by sailboarders. This will keep you from chilling down quickly, and may help you avoid hypothermia.

A final point. This section of the Sacandaga River is dam-controlled, which means that its water level is variable depending upon when and how much water is being released. Generally speaking, water is released on the weekends from Memorial Day through late June from about nine A.M. to five P.M., and every day during those hours in the summer. (During dry spells, the time that the dam is open may be shortened.) If you feel that the river seems incredibly shallow or sluggish, sit down on the shore and wait for a short while. Inevitably, another surge of water will be forthcoming—one that you'll be able to ride and enjoy without crashing into exposed rocks or getting stuck in the shallows.

On our last visit to the Sacandaga River, the stream was running high. Exhilarated, Barbara and I put our tubes in by the dam and pushed off from shore. At first, the current seemed lethargic. Then suddenly, as we pulled away from the shore, the force of water, moving at four thousand cubic feet per second, grabbed hold and swept us along.

Immediately, we raced through a short stretch of white water. Our initiation to the river had begun. Then, as quickly as they had started, the rapids were over, and we found ourselves floating leisurely along on serene ripples. The water seemed so tranquil in places that it was only by looking at the shore and glimpsing the trees racing by that we realized just how quickly we were traveling.

"Here's to Huckleberry Finn!" I called out to Barbara, who was floating only an arm's-length away. I put my hands behind my head and stretched out on the tube, lying horizontally across it. With the sun beating down, it was easy to forget just how swiftly the river was carrying us.

"Don't get too relaxed!" Barbara warned. "I can hear the approaching rapids."

Sure enough, with the sound drumming louder in our ears, we saw rapids dead ahead, coming quickly upon us.

"Get ready!" I shouted.

Suddenly, the water grew turbulent, as if we had been thrown into the maw of an enormous washing machine.

"Wheee!" Barbara cried out. We were really being bounced around now, and the sensation was like coming down from the top of the world's highest roller coaster.

"Whoa!" I yelled, as my tube was turned around by the turbulence. Before I knew it, I was heading downstream backwards. Using my hands as paddles, I quickly rotated the tube so that I was facing downstream again.

On we continued through the churning waters. Occasionally I could feel the jostle of a rock or boulder sliding beneath me.

And then, just as suddenly, the river turned calm, and for the moment, we had entered the eye of the hurricane. As we continued down the river, we watched several teenagers swinging out over the river on a long rope tied to an overhanging tree limb. When they reached the highest point of the swing, they let go, and then plummeted into the deepest part of the river.

Within a few moments, the teenagers had receded into the distance. After floating under a cable stretched overhead from shore to shore, we came to the most exciting part of the river, just outside of Hadley where the historic Bow bridge and train overpass were visible. At this point, the water really roared as we came down through the gorge. As Barbara and I shot through, the waves grew so violent that it was all that we could do just to stay on the tubes.

A word to the wise here—although being separated from your tube generally isn't life-threatening, particularly if you're wearing a life vest, it's best to get right back on your tube if you can. If you can't, remember to point your feet downstream to ride out the rapids. Keep your head up to watch where you're going and to avoid being struck by a rock.

I'll never forget the time I was tubing on the Esopus River in Phoenicia, down in the Catskills. In one huge drop, I was thrown off the tube and rolled over the boulders like a rag doll. With some effort, I got to the shore and pulled myself out. Glasses gone, knees bruised and bleeding, I felt like I had truly been put through the ringer. That's my worst experience white-water tubing, probably the result of my miscalculating and starting off when the water level was too low. Fortunately, nothing even remotely close to that has happened to me on the Sacandaga River.

If you do become separated from your tube, you must never try walking along the river bottom. Since the water is frequently three to five feet deep, it's very tempting to stand on the bottom and start walking. The danger, however, is that by making your way on foot, you could inadvertently step into a crevice between two rocks and get caught. If this should happen, the force of the water sweeping across you—at flood stage, it's strong enough to snap a canoe in half—could bend you over, forcing your face into the water. Over the last few decades there have been several deaths caused by just such circumstances. Paddlers, separated from their crafts, have stepped onto the slippery, rocky bottom, caught a foot and drowned when the current pushed them down while they were in only chest-deep water.

The last set of Sacandaga rapids can be tricky, and both Barbara and I have been thrown from our tubes by this violent water. On one occasion, I remember coming to the last grand stretch of cascades and noticing that a huge commercial raft was bearing down on me. They were moving at a much faster rate since there were many paddlers aboard. Although I could see that we were on a possible collision course, there was little I could do to alter the flow of events since it was my two flailing arms against their eight indomitable paddles.

Within seconds we were next to each other. Suddenly, a huge wave lifted the front end of the raft high in the air, and for a second, I thought that I was going to be pulled under it. Fortunately, at the very last moment, I was thrown clear, and the raft passed without further incident. I say this just to remind tubers to stay alert and be ready for the unexpected.

After the final rapids, a huge expanse of water waits to greet you—the confluence of the Sacandaga and Hudson Rivers. When you reach this junction, you'll begin to understand just how powerful the Hudson is. Although our goal has always been to make our way straight across to the opposite shore at the village of Lake Luzerne, Barbara and I generally find ourselves being swept downstream by the powerful current, away from the "Bridge of Hope" that spans the Hudson River between Hadley and Luzerne. Eventually, we do manage to get to that shore, but never without a struggle.

What's great about finishing the trip is that you're all set to do it again if you so choose. And many people do—over and over again.

THE GREAT SACANDAGA LAKE FROM A PARACHUTE

YUP. I ACTUALLY PARACHUTED FROM AN AIRPLANE AND GOT TO SEE THE GREAT SACANDAGA LAKE AS I FELL FROM 2,800 FEET

A number of years ago, I got the brilliant idea that I wanted to try something really different. This was before bungee jumping was popular, thank goodness. But what? One of the nursing staff at Ellis Hospital where I was working at the time was a fanatic at skydiving, and kept telling me that I should give it a try. Not wanting to look wimpy, I finally told her, "No sweat. Sign me up," and then convinced a coworker of mine, David, to make the pilgrimage with me.

That was how it all got started. David, his brother-in-law, Jim, and I headed up to the Drop Zone Parachute Club at the Fulton County Airport to take half a day's worth of parachuting lessons culminating in a static line jump, meaning that the chute is automatically deployed as you leave the plane.

We got to the airport, located on Route 67 just east of Johnstown, in the morning and proceeded to go through four hours of classes in which we were taught the basics of parachuting, including how to control your direction of flight as you descend, and how to hit (er, I mean "land on") the ground properly.

By the way, the impact of landing, if you do it right, is equivalent to jumping off the roof of your car; just don't try it if you own a huge tractor trailer.

Needless to say, we were all a bit nervous over the thought of doing an actual jump. After all, although I had been up in an airplane before, I had always ridden it back down. This was to be a different kind of experience—literally a one-way trip.

For a static line jump, there really isn't much you need to do the first time out. It's only later, when you start doing free-falls—meaning that you open your own chute at a predetermined altitude—that the training really begins to pay off.

The only thing I had to worry about was how to respond if I jumped, looked up, and noticed that my main chute had failed to open and was streaming above me like a roman candle. Now remember that we were jumping from 2,800 feet up, which meant there were only a few seconds to react before impact if something went wrong. Over and over again I had rehearsed in my mind what to do if I saw the main chute trailing above me: grab my reserve chute located on my chest, and throw it straight out from me so that it would open up as far away from the main chute as possible; otherwise, there would be the very real possibility that the emergency chute could tangle with the main chute, and I would be back to square one, with a life-threatening problem and no third chute as backup. In case you're prone to worry about such things, it's very rare that the main chute malfunctions; still, if it happens to you, the only thing standing between you and ending up flatter than a pancake are those four hours of training!

All of this crossed my mind as we finished the classes, practiced how to land doing a quick tumble or two from a small platform, and got suited up for the jump.

I can remember my mouth growing very dry at this point and the feeling of butterflies in my stomach; apparently my stomach was already airborne. As I recall, David and Jim didn't look so good either, despite their forced bravado.

As it turned out, the three of us were separated and ended up in different flight groups; consequently, we didn't have to maintain our false bravado, at least with each other.

However, the two jumpers who went up in the plane with me were both young women. Slowly, my bravado turned into resolve. Somehow I knew, then and there, that there was no way I wasn't going to jump, even though every fiber of my body wanted to stay on terra firma.

The flight up was uneventful. I got to listen to the jump-master and the pilot discuss some technical matters, like which of the summer blockbuster movies was the best one to see. After we had reached our designated altitude, the jump-master checked all of the equipment and our packs, and connected us to the static line that would automatically pull our chutes open as we left the airplane.

At near 3,000 feet, everything below began to acquire a surreal, toy-like quality, as if we were hanging over an enormous, flat canvass painting.

One of the women was the first to jump. That was good. Now there was one less witness just in case I backed out at the last moment. Surely, others before me had gotten cold feet and declined to jump but, then again, probably not too many. After all, the $60 charge (remember, this was years ago) was nonrefundable.

Suddenly it was my turn.

"Feet out!" the jump-master ordered.

Suspending rational thought, I swung my legs out through the doorway and partially put my weight onto the step below the door.

"Get out!" he commanded next.

Following a pre-understood program, I grabbed hold of the wing strut with my hands, stretched my body out, and found myself suspended horizontally between the wing strut and doorway step.

Arch your back I kept repeating to myself, wanting to strive for perfect form on my first jump.

The sound of the wind whipping around me was deafening.

I looked down, still not totally comprehending all of the new, mind-wrenching sensations my body was being subjected to.

"Go!" the jump-master shouted.

For a second I hesitated, and then I released my grip.

Suddenly, the roar of the wind vanished and the plane was gone, seemingly miles away in an instant. I was surrounded by total serenity, all in the matter of a split second.

I looked up, half afraid that I would see blue sky instead of an open chute. But there, above me, rocking in the breeze, was the white canopy of the parachute.

Everything was going fine.

At that moment, I knew that I was going to make it.

Suddenly, the two-way radio I was wearing crackled to life, breaking the serenity, and the ground instructor down at the airport began issuing directions on which way to steer the chute. The intent here was to ensure that I would land in a clear area by the airport. There were toggles to pull for controlling the direction of the parachute, one for each hand, and I did as the ground instructor ordered me to do, having no idea on my own exactly where I was heading.

For the next three minutes, I literally floated in a blissful state of ecstasy, watching the world below me gradually growing large. Off in the distance, to the northeast, I could see an enormous body of water which I later learned was the Great Sacandaga Lake. With the exception of the occasional crackle of my two-way radio, there were neither sounds nor distractions.

Soon I realized that I was coming down into an open field. I could see a man sitting on a motorcycle watching me descend. I found myself mesmerized by his silent presence.

Distracted, I suddenly realize that the ground was immediately coming up to meet my feet. At that moment, inexplicably, I totally forgot everything that I had learned in my training about how to land, and hit the ground hard, not even rolling. I immediately felt an excruciating pain in my left ankle, and went down in a heap. Still, I had the presence of mind to pull in my chute, lest the wind billow it and drag me ingloriously across the field.

Maintaining as much dignity as I could, I hobbled towards the main hanger, unable to bear any weight on my left foot.

Moments later, I reconnected with David and his brother-in-law. Jim had made an uneventful jump and was already making plans to return next week. David's jump had likewise gone well, except for a somewhat remarkable landing. He had overshot the main field by some distance and had come down between an old farm machine that would have sliced him into pieces like an egg slicer if he had landed on it, and some towering high tension wires. Furthermore, when David landed, he forgot to bunch up his chute. As a result, the parachute immediately filled with air and the wind dragged him some twenty to thirty yards across the field and left him tangled in a barb wire fence.

As for me, well, my ankle began to swell up, and I ended up going to the emergency room at Ellis Hospital for x-rays. I didn't break my ankle, but ended up having sprained it badly which, they say, can be even worse. For the next six weeks, I hobbled around using crutches, and then graduated temporarily to a cane.

But worst of all, I had to learn to live with a new nickname, which fortunately was short-lived, for every time David saw me coming, he would shout out, most embarrassingly "And here he is, folks ..... Mister Sky King!"

20,000 LEAGUES UNDER THE SAC

WHAT IS IT LIKE TO SCUBA DIVE UNDER THE GREAT SACANDAGA LAKE? FOR ONE THING, IT'S VERY MURKY AND COLD

"Stay loose. Relax!" I kept telling myself as I strove to make my respirations regular and even. After all, I was but a mere fifteen feet below the water's surface, gliding effortlessly along the sandy bottom of the lake with a full tank of oxygen strapped onto my back. If anything happened, I was only two strokes away from kicking up to the surface. Even so, a part of me couldn't help but feeling uneasy about the unnatural experience of breathing under water.

I looked over to my right and squinted through the murky depths. I could faintly see Barbara, my wife-to-be, accompanied by one of the diving instructors, moving through the same sandy waters several yards away. For whatever it was worth, she looked about as relaxed as I was feeling.

Yes, here we were—20,000 leagues under the Sac—right off of the public beach by the half mile long Batchellerville Bridge. At the time, neither of us knew anything about the Great Sacandaga Lake other than it was where we had come to do our open water dive in order to be certified in scuba diving. Up to that point, our association with scuba gear and diving conditions had been confined to the clear, warm, safe waters of the indoor swimming pool at the Cohoes Community Center.

Upon arriving at the Great Sacandaga Lake that day, we realized all too quickly that the waters of the Sacandaga were anything but warm or clear or inviting! This fact became abundantly clear when necessity forced us to squirm into 3/8 inch thick, neoprene wet suits for protection from the coldness—an acknowledgment that the body loses heat twenty-three times faster in water than in air, particularly when you are totally immersed.

Propelling myself along, a brief smile flickered across my face as I recalled how we all had looked on the shore. By the time I had gotten into my wet suit, put on the fins (or flippers as I prefer to call them), strapped on the oxygen tank, and adjusted the regulator, I was feeling more like Godzilla than an inept human waddling before the crowds. The stiff neoprene wet suit created just enough resistance to make all movement somewhat more labored.

"My body feels like lead," I heard Barbara moan as she got up onto her feet. She drooped visibly from the weight of the oxygen cylinder on her back and, like me, walked with the same ungainly duck-stride.

Making matters worse, we were encumbered by prodigious weight-belts around our waists, ensuring that we wouldn't come bobbing back up to the surface like a cork once we went down. Although a drowning person would beg to differ, the human body actually possesses quite a bit of lift to it in the water. Add to that a buoyant wet suit and a tank of air, and it can be quite difficult to stay on the bottom without a weight-belt and buoyancy compensator.

"You look nice in black today," I kidded Barbara, trying to come up with something positive to say about her lackluster looking wet suit.

Barbara didn't look any too happy at my comment.

"And you look like the Creature from the Black Lagoon," she shot back without a moment's hesitation.

I was about to attempt a witty retort, but was stopped in mid-sentence...

..."All right gang, listen up!" our diving instructor, Frank, suddenly bellowed out, cutting through the nervous chatter. The whole group of us, neophytes to the last, gathered around and listened intently as Frank reviewed procedures and protocols. This was information that had been repeatedly drilled into our heads during a succession of evenings spent in the swimming pool at the Cohoes Community Center.

First of all, everyone was to have a "buddy"—that's what you call someone who has sworn with uplifted right hand (and fingers crossed, no doubt) that they will watch your back if you promise to watch theirs. Scuba diving, you see, is similar to rock climbing in that your life may depend upon the reflexes and good judgment of the person you're paired up with. Get a bad *buddy* and you could end up as a *body* if something goes wrong.

At least none of us needed to worry about decompression tables; we were all going to remain in fairly shallow waters for the entire open water dive. If you descend deeper than thirty-three feet, however, and stay down for an extended period of time, then you have to be wary of a condition known as the *bends*, or decompression sickness, which is the result of coming up too quickly. This happens when bubbles of nitrogen gas precipitate into your blood stream, causing intense pain and even death if the bubbles happen to block off blood flow to a vital organ. To prevent the bends, all you need to do is to return to the surface in stages, stopping at different depths to give the nitrogen gas a chance to be reabsorbed by the body,

Fortunately, the Great Sacandaga Lake is seventy-five feet at its deepest, and only reaches this depth when the reservoir is filled to full capacity, generally in the early spring, and you happen to be directly above the original bed of the Sacandaga River. It is not a lake where depth is typically a serious concern.

I breathed a sigh of relief as Frank continued on methodically, reviewing underwater hand-signals, pressure gauge readings, operating the purge valve, and so forth.

"And if you go looking for underwater treasures, don't get trapped inside an old wreck," he ended with a joke, knowing full well that the GSL has no maritime history associated with it—and for good reason. The lake's only existed since 1930.

"Now let's scuby do!"

Into the water we shuffled, walking backwards due to the long fins on our feet that prevented forward ambulation. Twenty feet out from shore, the water finally became deep enough for us to topple in backwards, twist around, and begin swimming away from the beach. Although the temperature of the water was a frigid sixty degrees, the coldness quickly vanished as the thin envelope of water between the wet-suit and our skins warmed up.

As usual, I was amazed at how light and unencumbered I felt once I was totally immersed in the water. A few adjustments on the buoyancy compensator, and I had attained *neutral buoyancy*—a state where you neither sink downward nor rise upward. Floating about weightlessly in the water, with no inherent up or down, it was easy for me to imagine how astronauts must feel working in outer space under conditions of zero gravity.

Scuba diving in the Sac, however, is not as visually exciting as you might at first expect. To begin, the water is so murky that you can barely see more than seven or eight feet ahead of you—a fact that applies to nearly all bodies of water in the northeastern United States. Secondly, there is nothing particularly noteworthy to look at anyhow, even if you could see further; just large expanses of sand and mud, with clumps of weeds, an occasional stump, and rocks scattered about.

To be sure, there are several underwater sites around the Great Sacandaga Lake that are more visually stimulating, particularly where relics from the pre-reservoir days can be found, such as old foundations, roadways, fence posts, railroad tracks, and bridge abutments. These artifacts generally can be discovered in areas where communities once flourished—villages such as Fish House, Cranberry Creek, Munsonville, Day, Batchellerville, and Sacandaga Park.

On my initial dive, however, the impression of the Great Sacandaga Lake was of an underwater desert.

The first part of the open water dive—namely, demonstrating basic competency in underwater maneuvers—went without a hitch. Probably the trickiest part was taking off our face masks underwater, putting them back on, and then purging the masks of water so that we could see again. Although not all that difficult to do once you master the technique, it can be a bit intimidating at first, for not only does the face mask, once it is filled with water, cover your eyes, but your nose as well!

We also did a few exercises involving *buddy breathing*. This was fairly straightforward, and no more difficult than passing a peace pipe back and forth between you and your partner; only in this case what you inhale is air. If nothing else, it's a good exercise in learning to trust another person with your own personal well-being.

The only problem I had during underwater maneuvers involved *equalization*. No matter how hard I blew my nose or tried chewing or swallowing, I was not able to equalize so that the air pressure inside my ear matched the water pressure outside. As a result, my eardrums were constantly hurting, and got worse the deeper I went since water pressure increases as a function of depth. Fortunately, we were in relatively shallow water, and I was able to continue the exercises with only mild discomfort.

Next we moved out towards the Batchellerville Bridge, where the water grew steadily deeper, so that we could practice emergency ascents. In essence, we would take turns descending to the bottom of the lake, a plunge of perhaps twenty to twenty-five feet at this particular spot, and wait for Frank to turn off our oxygen valve. The purpose of the exercise was to expose us to a potentially stressful situation so that we would learn the appropriate responses, the first being not to panic.

When you stop to think about it, being suddenly unable to breathe under water is about as stressful as it gets. The correct response to a no-oxygen crisis, in case you're wondering, is to kick like crazy to get to the surface of the lake. If you're so far below the surface that decompression is required, a proper hand signal to your partner (hand extended under your throat) will hopefully elicit a cooperative response, and you'll buddy-breath for a while until you can make your way carefully up to the surface.

Despite my anticipatory jitters, I'm happy to report that everything went well. Frank turned off my air supply, I waited until I noticed I was without oxygen, which happened almost immediately, and then I kicked right up to the surface of the lake without the slightest hesitation. I didn't even feel short of breath, and there's a good reason why. The lungs begin to expand as you come up from the deeper pressures, and you never quite run out of breath unless you linger to look at the fish.

As cars crossed over the Batchellerville Bridge, undoubtedly several drivers noticed the activity below and wondered what was happening. Perhaps a few thought we were dredging the lake looking for a body, since every year one or two people accidentally drown at the Great Sacandaga Lake and divers have to be called in to recover the victim. Little did they know that we were all novice divers, and that the only skin we were interested in saving was our own!

A month later I received my certification in scuba diving, and was also issued a PADI card, an acronym for Professional Association of Diving Instructors, which can be used anywhere in the world where equipment needs to be rented. The world all at once had become my oyster.

And as for the Great Sacandaga Lake, three years later it suddenly assumed new and even greater importance in my life when Barbara and I came to be married and to spend our summers up at the lake. Who would have imagined that such great things would come from the murky world of scuba diving?

Doing the Sac by Canoe

If you're willing to forgo power boats, canoeing the upper Sacandaga River is a water barrel of fun

There are many ways to explore the upper Sacandaga River—the main tributary of the Great Sacandaga Lake. While some folks enjoy adventuring on motorboats, party barges, or jet skis, invariably the two of us choose the path of least technology—the time-honored *canoe*.

But why muscle-powered over motorized crafts? I can't really say. It's just that for as far back as I can remember, speed, noise, and power have never been prerequisites for my having a good time; and, by a stroke of good luck, I married someone who feels the same way.

It was a forgone conclusion, then, that we would bring the old battered, but dependable, Grumman along, and it was just as well, for we later discovered that a motor boat would have lasted about two seconds before being immobilized by the seemingly infinite number of rocks and boulders that infest the shallow stream bed.

With canoe secured on to the top of our Mazda, we drove slightly over five and a half miles north on Route 30 from Northville, reaching a turn-off on our left that led immediately down to the Sacandaga River. This was our starting point.

We quickly unloaded the canoe, threw in our paddles, life jackets, and waterproof bag of provisions, and lugged everything down a steep embankment to the water's edge.

We were all set.

Except for one detail. How were we going to get back to the car after canoeing seven meandering miles? Clearly, the car was too big to bring along in the back of the canoe.

Barbara was not in the least bit worried. She had already grabbed a book to read, leaving me to solve the problem.

"All right," I mumbled as I put on my sweatband, and tightened up the laces on my running shoes. "See you in a while."

I jumped into the Mazda-mobile, and quickly drove back towards Northville until I reached the State Launching Site just north of the Northville

Bridge. With some fancy maneuvering, I found a parking spot in the midst of all the trucks and trailer-hitched vans, and then began the long jog back to the canoe and Barbara.

Unfortunately, what I hadn't counted on was just how hot the sun would prove to be, for it beat down on me unforgivingly as I hoofed it along Route 30 over its streaming, shadeless asphalt surface.

Forty minutes later I arrived at the launching site and joined up with Barbara. She was still engrossed in her book.

"What took you so long?" she asked, looking up as the pages began searing from the heat of my body.

"Water!" I gasped. "I need water."

Quickly, I threw myself into the stream and laid out flat across the shallow river bed, letting the current sweep over me. Simultaneously, I began gulping down welcomed slugs of water from a plastic bottle Barbara had tossed me.

After several minutes I was feeling much improved.

Not being one to waste time needlessly, I signaled my O.K. with a thumbs up, and exclaimed "Let's do it!" I pealed myself off the shallow river bed, jumped into the canoe with Barbara, and down the river we immediately proceeded.

The first mile or so took us over a series of shallow rapids with Class II waters. At one point, we encountered a section so lacking in depth that the rocks snagged the front of the canoe, spinning us completely around. We ended up facing upstream stuck on the rocks.

"This is not going quite as planned," I groaned, trying to push the canoe free with my paddle.

"Hold on a moment," Barbara replied. "I've got a better idea." Barbara looked at me cunningly. "Let's turn ourselves around inside the canoe."

We did, each turning 180 degrees so that now we were facing downstream, only with the canoe in reverse.

"O.K. Now push!" Barbara shouted, and as we worked in unison, the canoe came free, and quickly shot through the remaining rapids going backwards, but with us facing forward.

Once we hit the placid waters, we reversed ourselves in the canoe, and then turned the canoe around so that it was again facing downstream.

"Not bad," I admitted as we continued along, being a little more wary about the underlying rocks now.

After a short time we passed by an old farm house, and then several small, deserted cottages. Despite the occasional presence of civilization, the river still felt like a wilderness; that is, until we swerved east, and proceeded under the bridge where Route 30 crosses overhead. From here on, the character of the river began to change from semi-wilderness to hard-core civilization.

It was also shortly after this point, as we turned south again, that we suddenly encountered a wind of such ferocity that its force against our bodies was greater than the forward motion of the current. There was only one solution, and we buckled down, keeping our heads low, and really began paddling strenuously.

As we continued on, I could see more and more camps beginning to line the shore of the Sacandaga River. Then, unexpectedly, the river widened, becoming lake-like in size; and all at once we were being visited by an occasional boat.

It probably took us at least twenty minutes to canoe the length of this wide, lake-like section, the winds having died down somewhat. Then, once again, the waters narrowed, becoming a river once more, but much deeper now.

Gradually, more and more boaters began to make themselves known, whizzing constantly by us in both directions. We found ourselves having to be continuously on "red" alert in order not to be swamped by huge waves. On one occasion, when I wasn't paying close enough attention, it was only Barbara's sharp cry of warning that got me to react in time. A large speedboat had passed at some distance from us, generating a volley of huge waves in its wake. I quickly turned the canoe into the incoming waves just in time, and we went up and down repeatedly as though on a roller coaster.

Naturally, I proceeded to blame the speedboat captain and not my own inattentiveness for nearly getting swamped. "Canoe you!" I believe was what I yelled at the receding boat.

After another fifteen minutes, it became obvious that we were close to the boat launching site because the motorboats were now joined by jet skis, and the water was churning in all directions. All this time, we had hugged the shoreline as closely as we could without getting swamped by the waves as they broke in the shallow waters.

We hooked a right at the launching site, and brought the canoe in quickly.

Barbara let out a sigh of relief. The last mile or two really had been pretty intense, with a tremendous number of motorized traffic crisscrossing the river as we approached the main body of the Great Sacandaga Lake. Although there are huge sections of the river to canoe where motorboats and jet skis are not present, the part just above the Northville Bridge is clearly not one of them.

IN SEARCH OF KUNJAMUK CAVE

IS KUNJAMUK CAVE FOR REAL? SEE FOR YOURSELF

One of our earliest adventures occurred when we went off in search of the Kunjamuk Cave in Speculator. It just so happens that I had known about the Kunjamuk Cave for some time, but neither Barbara nor I had been able to acquire specific information about its physical appearance, dimensions, or formation. All we had to go on were some general directions for getting there, and the knowledge that it was possible to access the cave either on foot, by cross-country skies, or by canoe.

It was late fall when we headed up north on Route 30 to scenic Speculator— headwaters of the Sacandaga River. We arrived at the center of the village, and then turned right onto Elm Lake Road. From here we continued east for about a mile, and then parked off the road at the point where the pavement ended.

As we put on our hiking boots and backpacks, we noticed that few leaves remained on the trees and that the brightness and colors of autumn had long passed. Winter could not be too far ahead, and I remember saying to Barbara that even the geese were gone, and no longer flying across an invisible highway in the sky.

Continuing on foot from Elm Lake Road, we noticed that the hike soon became interestingly maze-like in character. Seemingly, there were an endless number of old logging roads to choose from. But which one led to the Kunjamuk River and the correct crossing?

It was at this point that we wished we could be Natty Bumpo and Chingachgook just for the afternoon. However, after much plodding and deliberation, we finally arrived at the Kunjamuk River, and at a spot where clearly something had spanned the river in the distant past. This was an important detail, you see, for I clearly remembered having read that an old footbridge used to cross the Kunjamuk River, but that the bridge had been destroyed either by flooding or the ravages of ice. We were on the right track!

However, there was one problem. A very big problem as it turned out! The Kunjamuk River stood in our way, and it looked at least fifteen feet wide at its narrowest, with the water growing increasingly deeper towards its middle.

"I'm going across!" I suddenly announced in a resolute voice.

"Who are you kidding?" Barbara exclaimed. "I bet the water is at least up to your neck."

Quickly, I analyzed my options. There was no way to pole-vault across, and there was no visible narrowing of the river either upstream or downstream to make for an easier crossing; however, the thought had occurred to me that if I were to strip down and carry my clothes in a bundle above my head, I might be able to wade across the stream.

I looked at Barbara and she at me.

"I think I can make it," I insisted. Clearly, I had become so fixated on completing the adventure that no little river was going to stand in my way.

"No way!" Barbara protested. "Come on, be reasonable. First of all, it's late fall and the air temperature is no warmer than forty degrees. The water's probably just as cold. Think about that for a moment. Secondly, how do you know the water isn't over your head near the middle of the stream? What are you going to do if it gets that deep—end up breathing through a reed?"

Barbara was really getting into it now. Like a prosecuting attorney she continued on, adding more weight to her argument. "And suppose you slip on the slimy rocks, losing your balance in the process, and go completely under, including all of the clothes you're carrying? What are you going to do then? Walk out of here soaking wet and get hypothermia?"

The hypothermia argument is always guaranteed to work with me. I hate being insufferably cold for any length of time!

Still, if I had been alone I know I would have gone ahead and done it—and probably have been none the worse off for it. However, with Barbara's words chipping away at my confidence, I finally lost my resolve and, with tail between my legs, slinked away from the river, trailing behind Barbara back to the car.

So ended adventure number one!

Adventure number two began in the middle of winter when we again returned to Speculator, this time armed with snowshoes. For some reason, long forgotten, we had elected not to use cross-country skis. Although the woods were filled with two to three feet of snow, the snowshoes kept us from sinking in, and gave us comparatively solid footing. As a result, it didn't take long for us to get back to the Kunjamuk River. This time, however, the path ahead was unimpeded. The deep freeze of winter had put down at least five inches of solid ice over the river.

Trudging ahead, we proceeded across the Kunjamuk River and up a slope called Cave Hill to a small glen where Kunjamuk Cave can be found. Despite everything being entombed by snow, we were able to find the cave entrance without much difficulty. Its black opening in the whiteness of snow stood out starkly. The opening was so big, in fact, that we were able to walk in without hardly stooping.

And then, twenty-five feet into the side of the hill, just as things were beginning to get exciting, the cave came to an abrupt end.

We were disappointed that the cave had petered out so quickly, but were otherwise enthralled, for we found ourselves standing in a rather large chamber, perhaps six feet wide and up to thirteen feet in height. It was a very adequate shelter from the elements!

"I guess we don't need flashlights or carbide lamps for this one," I remarked offhandedly. But it was true. There was so much light coming in the front entrance, and from a smaller aperture above resembling a skylight, that there was no need for any other sources of illumination.

Taking off our backpacks, we casually looked around.

The walls of the cave were surprisingly smooth and contoured. In fact, the cave seemed to be shaped like a huge capsule—a bubble in the side of the hill. One book we read had suggested several possible explanations for how the cave had formed. One theory hypothesized that the cave was man-made, having been dug out by prospectors looking for silver or gold. This was not a totally fanciful theory either. To the north across the Kunjamuk Valley, silver had actually been extracted from a mine on Dug Mountain.

"What do you think?" I asked Barbara. "Is the cave man-made, naturally formed, or blasted out by a UFO?"

Barbara shot me one of her quizzical looks, and then pondered the question for a moment.

"It's hard to say," she admitted, running her gloved hand over the unnaturally smooth walls of the cave. "This place reminds me of the pothole caves we once saw on Moss Island in Little Falls. My hunch is that the Kunjamuk Cave was carved out by eddies of water."

I agreed enthusiastically.

Of course, big deal! What do we know? Neither Barbara nor I are geologists. Still, if push comes to shove, I bet we're right on this one. Kunjamuk Cave looks exactly like what you would expect if it formed through the action of swirling waters, with stones grinding out and smoothing the walls of the cave.

There were no signs of human or animal tracks leading up to the cave, only our own. Truly, Kunjamuk Cave seemed remote and unvisited, at least in the winter. After eating a leisurely lunch, we packed up and left the protection of the cave. The trip back to the car took no longer than forty-five minutes.

Sometime later, I read in a more recent book that the Kunjamuk Cave is located on land owned by the International Paper Company. It would be best to get a permit from their Speculator Woodlands office, which is located just south of Speculator on old Route 30, before proceeding to the cave.

Happy spelunking!

Postscript

Since this article was first published, it would seem that Barbara and I ended up betting on the wrong horse. According to the experts, Kunjamuk Cave is not a naturally formed cave, but rather a man-made mine.

ISLAND HOPPING

JOIN US AS WE FURTHER EXPLORE THE ROCKS AND SHOALS OF THE GREAT SACANDAGA LAKE

In the spring of 1989, we were fortunate to acquire a tiny trailer home in the Sacandaga Trailer Park (owned and operated by Scott and Donna Lewis), and ended up enjoying the lake immensely, even though we were at some distance from it. In 1991, deciding to make a stronger commitment, we purchased a year-round cottage near Diamond Point, and found ourselves exactly where we wanted to be—right on the water's edge.

That same year, 1991, should be indelibly etched into the memories of all lake users, for it was the year that the Sac literally vanished before startled eyes. What happened was that unusually large volumes of water had to be sent downstate to push back the salty water coming up the Hudson from the Atlantic Ocean, and also to satisfy the power demands of nearby utility companies. With its waters being bled off, compounded by the general lack of rainfall that particular year to recharge the lake, the GSL slowly retreated further and further back, exposing huge areas of shore whose brown earth seemed to grow before us like a consuming desert. By mid-September, the beach extended so far out to the water's edge that it took Barbara and I over a minute to walk down just to take a dip.

"If this lake gets much lower," Barbara quipped on one particularly dry day, "we may need a dowsing rod to find it!"

At the same time, however, something was happening to counterbalance the loss of lake water—something truly remarkable! Islands were popping out of the lake all around us, seemingly from everywhere.

The first one to appear was Rock Island. Now, Rock Island has always been familiar to us by virtue of its proximity. It's located one-quarter of a mile straight out from our cottage and always makes an appearance every fall as the water level drops. For this reason, we had always thought of it as an isolate. But in 1991, almost before the words "Abra-Sacandaga" could be uttered, Rock Island at once cloned itself, and two sister islands emerged to the northwest and southwest of it!

Things were really starting to happen.

About two or three miles west of Rock Island, another body of sand emerged, which I presume must be a regularly appearing shoal, since it is listed on the navigational charts.

Around the same time, we also observed that a vague form between Rock Island and Sand Island was starting to grow under water, with several stumps first surfacing to herald the island's arrival. Within several weeks a huge, flat tract of land had broken through, creating what some of the old timers call *Stump Island*, presumably because of the tree stumps remaining on it. Within a short matter of time this island of sand had grown remarkably in size, many times more voluminous than Rock Island and the other shoals put together.

What made all of this fascinating for Barbara and me—offsetting the disappointment of seeing the lake gradually shrinking in size—was that the Sac now provided us with destinations to explore without the presence of competing boats, since most lake-users had taken their motorboats out of the shallow waters to avoid potential damage to their props.

Out from the basement of our camp came the canoe, kayaks, skijak, sunfish, and inner tubes. Into these non-motorized crafts went Barbara, myself, and all the friends we could gather together to form one huge fleet—the strangest flotilla you've ever seen!—to visit and explore the various islands.

Rock Island, due to its proximity, was the first on our itinerary. I would have to assume that Rock Island got its name because of its rocky mantle. In any case, the composition of the island never changed much as the lake level plummeted. It simply reared up higher and remained fairly compact. And the two companion islands? Well, they never evolved into anything more than essentially sandbars. For this reason, it didn't take us long to explore the entirety of Rock Island and its two satellites.

Onward we went over to Stump Island.

Now, Stump Island is massive. Even walking at a leisurely pace, it took us an appreciable amount of time to circumnavigate it by foot. I've already mentioned that the island undoubtedly got its name from the stumps clinging tenaciously to its tenuous sands. Still, this is only a guess. Maybe the name arose from the island's ability to "stump" people who try to find its location during the normal, high-water season. But when Stump Island shows itself, it is enormous. One of our friends commented that you could put a baseball field on the island and still have plenty of room to spare.

As we walked around, we saw several large boulders—remnants, I would presume, from the last glaciation. Those glaciers would have made wonderful house movers for sure! There was also one part of Stump Island on its eastern side where a huge drop-off could readily be found. One of our friends, ignoring my warning, stepped off from the sand bar thinking he would be in knee deep water, and found himself immediately treading water.

Sand Island, not surprisingly, had grown to epic size and proportions, easily doubling its size, and fanning out towards the eastern mainland where the waters between were very shallow. We were able to walk through chest-deep water from Sand Island to the mainland and back without much difficulty. Maybe indeed this was how the early settlers crossed the Bering Strait to America.

Later, as we strolled across the exposed southeastern side of Sand Island, we came upon the rocky ruins of an old foundation. All that remained was a rectangular outline. Even now, we still find it very hard to imagine an earlier time when whole towns, railroads, graveyards, farms and barns, and an amusement park once existed where the silent, unspeaking waters of the GSL now splash and tumble.

It was now time to turn around. We had put in a full day exploring the mid-range islands and shoals of the lake southeast of Diamond Point, and it was time to hit the sack.

Tomorrow we would surely hit the "Sac" again!

THE CALL OF THE KUNJAMUK

THE KUNJAMUK RIVER IS ONE OF THE SACANDAGA RIVER'S MAIN TRIBUTARIES

If you proceed north on Route 30 from Northville, you will quickly observe that the Great Sacandaga Lake turns into the Sacandaga River, which is the lake's main tributary and namesake. Continue further north, and you will eventually reach Speculator, where you can visit Pleasant Lake—the lake source for the Great Sacandaga Lake, and site of an attractive public beach.

Just before you get to the village of Speculator, however, you will reach a marshy, water-filled area to the east of Route 30 called Kunjamuk Bay, which is formed by the confluence of the Sacandaga River and the Kunjamuk River. It was from here that Barbara and I began a wonderful canoe journey up the Kunjamuk River—the inspiration for the trip coming from Alec C. Proskin's book *Adirondack Canoe Waters: South & West Flow.*

The Kunjamuk River, whose name is of unknown origin, is over seventeen miles in length, and rises from South Pond on the northern foot of South Pond Mountain. We were only planning to canoe to Elm Lake, which involved a round trip of seven miles—a sufficient distance for an afternoon adventure.

Using our newly acquired canoe carrier to wheel the canoe down to the lake, we were off and gliding across the smooth, silky waters of Kunjamuk Bay within a matter of minutes. In another five minutes we had crossed the bay, and readily found the mouth of the Kunjamuk River. All was going as planned.

As we headed upstream, we looked forward to a peaceful, easy paddle, since we already knew in advance that the elevation change was a scant four feet between Kunjamuk Bay and Elm Lake. There would be no rapids or small cascades to negotiate.

What the river did provide in abundance, however, was a tremendous sense of wilderness penetration and remoteness, even though this feeling was somewhat illusionary due to the invisible presence of Elm Lake Road, off to our left, as it paralleled the river. The only time we knew of the road's presence was when we had to go under a bridge that led over to one of its two secondary roads.

What we didn't expect, however, was just how snake-like and sinuous the river would be, with its unremitting U-turns, double S's, and constant jostling back and forth.

"I believe this river has more curves than Pamela Anderson," I joked, seeing if I could get a reaction from Barbara.

She just winced. "Since you brought up the subject, why is the Kunjamuk so curvy to begin with? I mean, we've been on the Mohawk River, boated on the Hudson River, and both are comparatively as straight as an arrow."

"You're right," I replied. "Perhaps the Kunjamuk, unlike some bad politicians, just doesn't know that it's crooked."

Barbara groaned.

"In all seriousness though," I continued, doing my best to make amends, "smaller rivers don't have as much power behind them as the larger ones, so they can't push their way as easily through obstacles, such as outcroppings of resistant bedrock. This means, then, that smaller rivers take the path of least resistance, and veer around areas of durable rock, forming winding pathways like the ones we're seeing."

Who knows if what I said is technically true, but it sounded good.

"I still don't understand why the path of least resistance can't be a straight line," Barbara grumbled to herself as we careened again into the opposite bank while trying to negotiate a sharp U-turn.

To me, the trip up was the equivalent of traveling through a botanical garden, with fields of yellow water lilies, purple pickerel weeds, red osiers, wild primroses, and other flowers and weeds too numerous to mention.

Occasionally, we had to push our way through one or two inch high dams created by fallen branches. In one instance, a one foot high beaver dam loomed ahead, but its northern end had been breached, and we were able to get through without having to portage the canoe.

When we came to the first bridge, which happens to be about halfway up to Elm Lake, we got out to stretch our legs, and to scamper up to Kunjamuk Cave, a well known land mark which is located on private land. (For further details, see the chapter, *In Search of Kunjamuk Cave*.) Note: you may first need to get a permit from the International Paper Company in order to visit the cave.

Back on the river we continued our paddle upstream. A short distance further we came to an area on our right where a huge slab of sloping rock descended into the stream. What we found of particular interest were two iron chains bolted securely into the boulder—fixtures you might see used to moor a large boat or yacht. Try though we may, Barbara and I couldn't come up with any convincing explanation as to what these bolts and chains were once used for on the Kunjamuk. It just didn't seem reasonable that anyone would have gone to all that work simply to tie up a canoe, for the fact of it is that no large boats could possibly have reached the point that we had paddled to!

As we negotiated bend after bend of winding river, we suddenly came upon a party of four in two canoes who were coming from the opposite direction. The man in the lead canoe indicated that he had been on the Kunjamuk five other times, and that this was the first time he had ever seen anyone else paddling its waters. I took this to be a good sign; namely that the Kunjamuk is not yet being over-utilized and loved to death.

"Look!" Barbara yelled joyfully from the bow of the canoe, long after we had passed the other canoeists. "Elm Lake is coming into view."

We had reached the 3.5 mile mark, but felt almost a sense of disappointment now that the end of the first half of the trip had been reached. Since Elm Lake is 0.8 miles long, we decided to canoe half way up its length just to look around more fully. On both sides of us, the lake waters extended into lush areas of swamp bushes and water lilies.

In certain respects the lake seemed more like an enormous marsh, with the river running through its middle, literally bisecting it.

We stopped paddling and Barbara, very carefully, turned 180 degrees around in the canoe so that she was facing me. It was time to break out the midday lunch, and we ate heartily while enjoying the changing views as our canoe responded to the pull of the river and wind, and slowly turned and circled downstream.

Off to the north, East Mountain, well over 2,600 feet in height, framed the lake against the sky.

We soaked in the views as we replenished ourselves on ham and cheese sandwiches. The only momentary crisis was the discovery that we didn't have a cork screw to open the wine bottle. Fortunately, Barbara, using her Swiss Army knife, was able to save the day.

Barbara turned around to face the bow again and we resumed paddling, this time wending our way down the way we had come up. With the wind at our backs, and the feeble current now going favorably in our direction, we were back at Kunjamuk Bay in what seemed like no time at all.

Once again, we were struck by the fact that canoeing is not only good for your soul, but the equivalent of taking a pleasant journey back into time, returning you to bygone days when birch canoes and compact boats were how early settlers and natives crossed the rugged north country.

HUSTED LAKE

HUSTED LAKE STILL EXISTS, EVEN IF YOU CAN'T SEE IT

Back in the days when the GSL was not a reservoir but rather an expansive valley, the village of Broadalbin was a favorite summer retreat for downstate New Yorkers. The famous writer and illustrator, Robert W. Chambers, and philanthropist, Katherine (Kitty) Husted, built impressive homes in Broadalbin which exist to this day, and helped to contribute to the village's growing economy.

In an earlier chapter, *Italian Gardens of Broadalbin*, I made mention of how the Italian Gardens were fashioned by Katherine Husted. Husted also created a small body of water that later came to be know as Husted Lake; and like the Italian Gardens, it gradually fell into obscurity.

My interest in Husted Lake began after seeing an old postcard which depicted a sizable looking pond located right in the village of Broadalbin. I had driven through Broadalbin on numerous occasions and had never once seen any body of water other than the Great Sacandaga Lake. "Could Husted Lake still exist?" I wondered to myself.

After consulting an old topo map, I was able to discover the past location of the lake—east of the village, bounded by Main Street to the west, Maple Avenue to the north, Mill Street to the east, and Bridge Street to the south. Was it still there, however?

To satisfy my curiosity, I slowly drove up and down these four roads, craning my neck for a look. It became quickly evident that Husted Lake, if it still existed, could not be seen from roadside, there being too many intervening private homes and buildings, such as the Mohawk Furniture Company. In addition, there clearly was no direct access to the lake without crossing private lands.

And so matters dropped for several years. In August of '95, however, an ingenious idea popped into my head. Why not canoe down the Kennyetto Creek to where Husted Lake was depicted on the map, look around, and then exit further downstream by Bridge Street.

I waited until several days of rainfall had swelled up Kennyetto Creek, and then put in my old fiber-glass kayak by the bridge at the intersection of Maple Street and Mill Street.

"I'll see you at the old railroad station in about an hour," I called out to Barbara, referring to the antique store that now occupies what was once the Broadalbin railroad depot. I had elected to take the solo kayak instead of the canoe for practical reasons; the stream didn't look deep enough to float the larger canoe with the weight of us two in it.

"Good luck," Barbara called out as I drifted away and started down the creek. She probably figured I needed it.

Sure enough. Within several minutes, my progress was abruptly halted by the first of several major barriers I would encounter—an old dam that stretched across the entire length of the river and which diverted part of Kennyetto Creek into an artificial channel, which then continued along the east side of Mohawk Furniture, over a small dam, and finally back out into Kennyetto Creek. This waterway, incidentally, is on private property and off limits to boats.

There was nothing I could do except portage the kayak around the north side of the dam, and this with some difficulty.

Oh, well. Nobody said this was going to be easy.

The dam itself stood over six feet high and had wooden slats stuck in along its top so that the amount of water released could be controlled. The slats were most visibly bent inward near the middle of the dam where the water pressure evidently was the strongest.

Once below the dam I set the kayak back into the stream and again was swept along by the rapid flow of water. The stream slowly began to meander and became bounded by an earthen bank, some three to four feet high, topped by thickets of dense vegetation and bushes. Suddenly it seemed like I was paddling down the Congo.

At one point a flock of ducks scurried across the water ahead of me, visibly annoyed that their sanctuary had been invaded. Soon after, the way ahead again became blocked by what at first looked like a beaver dam, but which ended up being an area of blow down. Getting around this obstacle proved to be laborious. But not so for the ducks who had moved off again as I approached.

Onward I continued until, five or ten minutes later, I noticed the Mohawk Furniture Factory coming into view on my left, and the backs of several buildings and homes on Main Street looming above me to the right.

Believe it or not, I had taken the entire trip down the Kennyetto Creek, and had missed Husted Lake completely!

Feeling annoyed and genuinely puzzled, I exited the stream near the old Railroad Station, all the while complaining to Barbara that I had gone the entire distance, roughly one, sinewy mile, and had never seen any evidence, past or present, of the lake.

Already I had summarily concluded that Husted Lake no longer existed. Maybe it was dam-created, and came to an abrupt end when the dam gave way, draining out all the lake waters and returning the stream to its channel. The only problem was that I had seen no evidence of such a dam on my journey.

Still, it sounded plausible—that is, until I studied my old topo map later that night, and picked up on something I hadn't paid attention to earlier.

"Look at this," I pointed out to Barbara. "Kennyetto Creek runs closely around Husted Lake but never through it."

That's why I had missed the lake.

Barbara nodded her head in agreement. "You're going to have to leave the stream to get to the lake," she said. "There's no other way to do it."

After studying the map more closely, it was evident that a waterway from Kennyetto Creek to Husted Lake existed, but one which had to be pretty tiny and inconspicuous, since I had missed it completely in my journey down the creek. The map also showed that a tiny channel led to Husted Lake from the east, off of the artificial channel near Mohawk Furniture, but this was clearly off limits since private land would have to be crossed to get there.

Obviously, all I had to do was go back upstream from where I had exited, look for a tiny channel off to my right, and it would lead me to the lake.

Once again, I headed into Broadalbin. This time I put the kayak in at the bridge on Bridge Street and kayaked upstream for 0.2 miles.

Sure enough, going off on my right, not too far upstream from the Mohawk Furniture Factory, was a tiny unnavigable channel. I pulled the kayak up to the edge of the bank, and then waded up the swampy channel by foot. (Well, it was a lot easier than trying to fight my way through the tangle of bushes along both sides of the channel.)

After fifty feet or so, stone walls appeared on the sides of the channel, which rapidly turned into a sluiceway, and then all at once I was at the top of a tiny dam's spillway.

And there, at the top of the dam, much to my delight was Husted Lake, and much larger and deeper than I had ever imagined it would be.

Immediately, my thoughts went back to 100 years ago when the lake was a major recreational attraction, complete with bath houses, a swinging suspension bridge which crossed over the creek to the lake, and swan shaped paddle boats. How times had changed. The lake was now home to whatever creatures chose to inhabit it.

Take note that Husted Lake is on private property, and that you may need to get permission even if accessing the lake from Kennyetto Creek.

SCOUT ISLAND

EXPLORING THE SOUTHERN END OF THE GREAT SACANDAGA LAKE

"Is this really the same lake?" Barbara asked incredulously as we canoed from one sandbar and minuscule island to the next one near Scout Island. Up to this point in time, our paddling adventures had been restricted to the area between Sand Island and the Kenyon Group.

"If it isn't, we're in trouble," I replied as we glided through dark waters. It reminded me of a Star Trek episode in which the crew of the Enterprise was instantly transported to a different quadrant in the galaxy, and found the stars and clusters before them totally foreign and unrecognizable.

Fortunately, we were still on the Great Sacandaga Lake, and not the victims of instant teleportation to uncharted waters. We had grown weary, you see, of exploring the same old area by our camp, and had come down to McMurray's Bay, six miles to the south, to rent a canoe and check out new horizons.

What intrigued us about the southeastern end of the lake was the significant number of small islands and sandbars—many of which are not even listed on the topo map—and Scout Island, the largest body of land on the lake. There was much to explore.

The smaller islands that we visited, however, were little more than patches of land with a smattering of trees and sprouts of grass—nothing to get too excited about, since ten large steps would take you across to the opposite side.

But Scout Island—now that was something different!

Scout Island is owned by the Boy Scouts of America, which is how it came to be named. It is also the island with the highest elevation—at least 800 feet above sea level—with a huge spine running north to south roughly along its center.

The only traces from the past Sacandaga Valley remaining on the island are a series of rock boundaries running perpendicular to each other. There are no buildings, and little else to show that the island has ever been occupied; just a flag pole on the northeastern section near the water.

Scout Island, it should be emphasized, is posted, meaning *no trespassing*, but you can certainly canoe around it.

Mr. McMurray, the affable, elderly gentleman who owns and operates McMurray's Livery and Launching site, told us that he remembers Scout Island from the days of his youth, before the valley was flooded, and before time had erased most of the valley's pre-reservoir history. At that time there were two farms on what is now the land constituting Scout Island; both were leveled to make room for the lake.

Although the trees may look centuries old—the proverbial *forest primeval*—the trees on Scout Island, and those on the other islands as well, are all new growth. In the late '20s, before the land was inundated, "cutters" swept through the valley, slashing away at all animate and inanimate objects, and reducing them to a height of no greater than twelve inches. What you currently see is the growth of over seventy years, with Scout Island having completely reforested itself.

To be sure, Scout Island has not always been unoccupied, even after the valley flooded. An early owner brought sheep onto the island, figuring that he'd use the lake as a natural boundary to keep the animals herded. All went as planned except for one thing—too many people were stealing the unguarded sheep, and the owner finally had to give up the business.

We canoed the area for three hours, and then returned to McMurray's Bay. After arriving, I asked Mr. McMurray about a huge circular piece of stone which I had seen lying in shallow waters, and which I took to be a cistern. According to McMurray, however, the object was the foundation for an old silo abandoned by one of the leveled farms. Obviously you can tell that I'm no farmer!

Mr. McMurray generously gave us several old postcards showing Scout Island and various parts of the bay as they looked in the early days after the reservoir had been created. We left, returning to our camp with a warm glow, feeling that the southern part of the GSL was no longer as unfamiliar to us.

Canoeing Kennyetto Creek

The Next Time You're in Broadalbin, Bring Along a Canoe

Although you may not know the Kennyetto Creek by name, you have undoubtedly crossed over it many times on your way through Broadalbin and Vail Mills, for there are no less than five bridges spanning the creek between Broadalbin and Mayfield; and while the Sacandaga River may be the largest tributary to the Great Sacandaga Lake and its namesake, Kennyetto Creek is by far its second largest tributary, and therefore worthy of consideration in its own right.

Don't think that canoeing the Kennyetto's going to be a picnic, however. Like any small to medium size stream, Kennyetto Creek offers areas of blow-down that have to be negotiated, and sections so shallow that rocks will literally grab hold of the canoe and not let go. To paddle the Kennyetto, you must be willing to portage where necessary, and to occasionally maneuver the canoe over areas of rocks and boulders. Neither of these inconveniences, however, are all that demanding and may, in fact, add to the overall sense of adventure.

The Kennyetto begins its journey in the distant hills northeast of Broadalbin, but we only need to concern ourselves with the part that starts at Broadalbin and flows into the Great Sacandaga Lake. The creek is so sinuous that the Indians named it *Kennyetto*, or "the snake that swallows its tale," and it is at Vail Mills that Kennyetto Creek becomes its most serpentine. Here, flowing southwest, the creek suddenly does an about face and proceeds northeast, entering the Great Sacandaga Lake at its south-most corner.

The best spot to put the canoe in is just below the bridge at Bridge Street. You will notice a mill upstream from the bridge, and the old

Broadalbin Train Station, now an antique shop, just downstream. Although the water is very shallow by the bridge, it quickly deepens once you put in and start paddling downstream, going west. As you canoe past the old train station, take note that you will be following the tracks of the Fonda, Johnstown & Gloversville railroad (the FJ&G) to your left.

Very soon you will pass under the South Second Avenue Bridge (another put-in point) and, still further on, the Route 30 bridge in Vail Mills. It is at this point that the creek begins to twist and to change direction dramatically, so that by the time you have circumnavigated the Adirondack Animal Land Park, you are now traveling northeast back towards the Great Sacandaga Lake. It is also at this point that the ghostly bed of the FJ&G Railroad disappears, continuing further west and then north.

When you reach the second Route 30 bridge crossing the Kennyetto Creek between Vail Mills and Sand Hill Road, you are not far from the Great Sacandaga Lake. A shallow river bed, however, may force you to walk or carry the canoe over short sections if you are canoeing in the middle of the summer when the water level is down.

Take heart, however, for the Great Sacandaga Lake, as you come into Muscle Bay, is a sight to behold, with its jagged shoreline and procession of large islands including Scout Island—the largest one on the lake.

Hopefully, you have thought ahead, and have a second car ready at the end of your trip; otherwise, it's time to turn the canoe around and retrace your route over each carry-out, stretch of blow-down, and shallow rock garden; a prospect that may not be quite so inviting in reverse!

A Field Trip to the Feldspar Mine

Another Adventure into the Hills above the Sacandaga Valley

In the upper reaches of the Mayfield Hills is a short hike up to the old, abandoned Feldspar Mine. We found it in Barbara McMartin's book, *Discover the Southern Adirondacks*, and were immediately intrigued.

Still, it took Barbara and me two separate outings before we were able to locate the mine—the difficulty arising, in part, from the myriad of logging roads and jeep trails that have infiltrated the woods over the last decade or two.

The climb up to the Mayfield Feldspar Mine involves an ascent of roughly 660 feet, and begins at a sand pit off of Mountain Road, approximately 1.4 miles north of the intersection of Mountain Road and Cross Road. Although McMartin talks about following a series of logging roads up to the mine—there being no direct route, unfortunately—the real secret lies in following the stream slightly north of the sandpit, and using it as a directional.

By staying close to the creek as you proceed uphill, you will eventually enter a large ravine which leads to the Feldspar mine. (This approach, however, may entail crossing private land, so get permission first.)

There are several key points to consider before undertaking this adventure. First of all, the feldspar mine is actually an open pit, and not an enterable shaft leading into the side of a hill. Secondly, the mine has been abandoned for quite a few years, with the forest essentially reclaiming the area. This means, then, that trees dominate the landscape, making it difficult to shoot a clear picture of the open pit if photography is your main interest.

Even though the area is gradually turning into wilderness, the feldspar mine remains an interesting destination for exploration, for it takes you back to the industrial age of the Sacandaga Valley—to the late 1800s and early 1900s, when nearby Sacandaga Park was flourishing as a tourist center, and the Fonda, Johntown & Gloversville Railroad provided transportation for both passengers and materials from the Mohawk Valley up to as far as Northville.

It was during this time period that the feldspar mine operated, excavating pink orthoclase feldspar and transporting it to a gravity-fed mill near Cranberry Creek, and by railroad to factories in New Jersey, where it was ultimately pulverized and used as china glaze. The mine ceased operations in the 1920s.

By visiting the open mine, you can see the excavated pit, with walls of feldspar partially obscured by abundant growths of green moss that seem to thrive on the dampness of the ravine. You will also see other igneous rocks, such as mica and quartz.

If you keep your eyes open you will notice several cement blocks nearby. In earlier days, these pillars supported the upper housing of a conveyer belt that led downhill to the FJ&G Railroad.

The FJ&G Railroad no longer exists, except for an abandoned section under the Great Sacandaga Lake, but you can still see the old FJ&G Railroad station at Sacandaga Park. For the last fifteen years it has been used as an art studio by Lawrence Faust, a local artist, but the exterior still looks very much the same as it did in the old days.

It just goes to show that pieces of the Sacandaga Valley's history remain to be seen, if you know where to look.

SANDBAGGED OFF SAND ISLAND

NEVER UNDERESTIMATE THE TENACITY OF A LAKE RANGER

The Great Sacandaga Lake is a great lake for adventures, just as it is for misadventures. The two of us know, since we seem to have a knack for getting our share of both. Our earliest incident occurred in late August of '92, at a point not too far off of Sand Island.

To begin, I should mention that there are sailors who reject all forms of motorized boats, and make use of self or wind-powered sailing crafts. These sailors can always be found in kayaks, sailboats, canoes, or on windsurf boards. Then there are sailors who love big party barges, speedboats, or jet skis. For them, the excitement is in racing ahead as fast as humanly possible, or in reaching a particular destination with the maximum expediency.

Then there are the *hybrids*—people who do both. We became hybrids in late August, but not before we ran head on into an adventure that we'll carry with us for a long time.

You see, up until late August, Barbara and I had been purists. No power boats or jet ski motors sounding like chain saws for us; only the silent contentment of wind and muscle for propulsion. Unfortunately, resorting to canoes, kayaks, and sunfishes ultimately condemned us to a small patch of lake in front of our summer camp near Diamond Point. With growing pangs of exploratory hunger, we began longing to savor the whole lake—not just one part of it.

Finally, we knuckled under, swallowed our purist pride and, as Barbara so aptly put it, became "ya-ho-ers" ourselves. Buying a five-horsepower motor was the easy part. The difficult part became using it. We owned a *Snark Wildflower*—a small sailboat—which we had purchased years ago through an advertisement in the Want-Ad Digest. The previous owner had been a purist as well; consequently, the Wildflower, like a wild horse, had never been saddled with a motor before. We would have to be the first!

Making matters worse was the fact that we had never been given any papers of ownership. We were without a title. Up until now this had not been a problem, since you don't need a registration in order to operate a non-motorized boat. However, as soon as you put a motor on it, no matter how small the boat or motor is, it becomes a motorized vehicle and subject to the maritime version of the Department of Motor Vehicles' rules and regulations.

As we milled around on the beach with our unregistered boat and untested motor, we knew all of this. At the same time, we had an uneasy feeling that maybe the motor didn't work as properly as it should, or that the propeller shaft wasn't long enough for the transom. There was only one solution; take the boat out for a trial spin before going through the hours of grief and aggravation at the Department of Motor Vehicles trying to register it.

Now, we have been out on the lake many times and I had never once in all my trips seen a patrol boat—*Smoky on the Water*, so to speak. In fact, encountering the lake police seemed to carry the same degree of probability as getting struck by lightning, sucked up by a tornado, or having a date with Christy Brinkley, although the latter would be quite endurable, I assure you. Consequently, throwing all caution to the wind, we hitched up the motor to the boat, revved it up, and headed out of the bay to give the engine and boat a thorough trial run.

The motor and boat, I'm happy to report, performed admirably. To be sure, we weren't jetting along throwing out huge waves in our wake, but we were trolling about at a steady pace, and I felt infinitely satisfied.

The water was choppy, but despite the bouncing up and down, much like riding on a mechanical bull, we progressed out to the two-mile point from shore, not very far from Sand Island. So far so good! We had brought a lunch with us, so we relaxed, all the time enjoying the wind, sun, and waves.

It was when we were heading back to our camp that disaster struck! Literally out of nowhere, like a hawk exploding suddenly into view in front of its startled prey, a patrol boat was all at once upon us. Even to this day I have no idea where this officer came from. Maybe he surfaced from the depths after sighting us with a periscope.

"I don't believe this is happening!" I exclaimed to Barbara incredulously, talking in a stage whisper. Like a dream, a very bad dream, the whole thing had a sense of unreality to it.

Barbara merely shook her head and grimaced.

I waited a second and immediately the patrol boat was on our port side.

"Grab hold of the gunwale!" the officer shouted over the wind and thumping of the boats on the water and against each other.

I grabbed hold as best as I could. We were now joined together, at least for the moment.

"Any problem, officer?" I asked with feigned naïveté. Deep down inside I kept hoping that the officer would notice we weren't outlaws or ya-ho-ers and disappear in a puff of smoke.

"Do you have a current registration for this boat?" he asked, obviously not one to engage in small talk.

Naturally, not having NY_______ decals on the boat was a dead give away as to its unregistered status. The officer must have spied us from far away with binoculars.

"Well, er. . . not exactly," I confessed, figuring a straightforward approach was probably the best one. "But we were planning to register the boat. We were just testing it first."

The officer looked at me quizzically. "I think you've got your order of priorities reversed," he finally stated. "Don't you know that even if you take the boat out only ten feet from the shore you're still in violation of the law if the boat is unregistered?"

"Gee, really?" I replied, scratching my head in feigned surprise.

"Are you carrying life jackets?" he immediately asked, not giving us a moment to gain the advantage.

"Certainly," I answered, showing the officer the one positioned next to me, and pointing out the one Barbara was wearing.

"How about an anchor?"

No problem. I proudly displayed the anchor we had stowed in the bow.

"Flashlights?"

I bet he thought he had us on this one. Barbara immediately pulled out a flashlight from her trusty backpack.

"And a horn or a whistle?"

Once again Barbara reached into her backpack—a veritable "horn of plenty"—this time producing a whistle. She gave it one toot for good luck.

The officer eyed us curiously.

"How are we doing, officer?" I finally asked, hopeful that four out of five wasn't so bad.

"I have to write you out a ticket for operating an unregistered boat," he said, almost with regret in his voice. "But look at it this way, folks. The money from the fine will help pay my salary and the cost of keeping the lake safe."

He handed me the ticket. "Don't worry," he added. "It doesn't go on your driver's license."

Well, that was a relief to know.

"Also," the officer continued, "I'll be a nice guy and allow you to continue operating your motor so that you can get back to shore."

Barbara and I did a double take. Huh?

"That's mighty big of you," I whispered under my breath.

The officer waited until we had started up the motor, and then was off like a shot. For all I know, maybe he went back down to the bottom of the lake to patiently wait for his next victim.

We slowly puttered back to shore, all the time wailing and moaning about the injustices of the laws of probability.

When we got back to the beach, we scanned the lake horizon with binoculars. There were no boats in sight. Like Clint Eastwood's *High Plains Drifter*, the officer had vanished into the sunset.

SAILING AND BAILING

EVERYONE HAS A SAILING ADVENTURE TO TELL—AND WE ARE NO EXCEPTION

Sailing on the Great Sacandaga Lake is a lot of fun, even when the boat does things it's not meant to do! Like every sailor we have ever met, we also have a tale to tell—the day our boat turned into a submarine.

For us, sailing at dusk when the wind is howling, and the sun is hanging in the sky near the horizon like a red lantern, is the most exciting time to be out on the lake. Needless to say, we like to think of ourselves as masterful sailors, but the fact of it is that we are intermediates at best. There's an old saying that a little bit of knowledge can be a dangerous thing. This was never truer than for sailing, particularly when you are an intermediate.

Conditions looked favorable, i.e., the wind was blowing like a hurricane and the lake looked as though underwater mines were being detonated, so I suggested to Barbara that we go out for a quick sail. Barbara at first seemed a little reluctant; after all, the lake appeared to be more suitable for a suicide than a sail. Some, by the way, might refer to Barbara's hesitation as an exercise of good judgment.

Still, we had been cooped up all week due to the weather being unbearably calm, and on a previous sail, when all the leaves stopped rustling gently on the trees, we had ended up like Samuel Taylor Coleridge's ancient mariner, "as idle as a painted ship upon a painted ocean."

Consequently, it really didn't take much coaxing on my part to convince Barbara that our destiny awaited on the Great Sacandaga Lake. You see, Barbara likes a good adventure, too.

With a little bit of effort, we pushed our sailboat, a 12-foot Wildflower, across the beach, using logs for rollers, until the boat was in the water. The sailboat immediately began leaping around like a bucking bronco as it lost contact with solid ground. Barbara was already in the boat getting the lines (shrouds) and rudder ready by the time I got the boat back under control.

Since we launched directly into the wind from the east side of the lake, I walked the boat out about twenty feet from the shore. This was not very difficult to do since the water level drops very slowly as you proceed from the shore. At a crucial moment, mainly determined by how wet I wanted to get, I scampered over the gunwale into the boat, and Barbara hoisted the mainsail.

We took off as though we had been shot from a crossbow. Immediately, the realization hit us both—we had been out in winds before, but this was something totally different.

"How are we doing?" I shouted to Barbara over the wind and noise of the waves. I settled myself in to get the jib ready.

"Ask me again when this nightmare is over!" Barbara shouted back. All of her concentration was being directed on handling the boat.

The force of the wind on the mainsail was tremendous, and it was clear to me that Barbara was doggedly trying not to engage its full ferocity.

Obviously, it would not be a good idea to also hoist the jib. Naturally, without a moment's thought, I proceeded to do so.

Our rate of velocity now accelerated as the jib filled with air. We were really wailing along!

But simultaneously, things were rapidly getting out of control, even as our minds vainly tried to grasp exactly what was happening. Suddenly, and totally without warning, the front of the boat literally nose-dived straight into the lake. I could only utter an exclamation of astonishment as we went down vertically like a submarine doing a crash dive. Although we didn't realize it then, the wind had caught the sail full force, literally driving the bow straight into the water.

Water poured all over us as the Sacandaga suddenly turned into Niagara Falls. Then, all at once, we were back up above the surface again, only now with the boat half-filled with water.

I could hear Barbara asking the inevitable question that all competent sailors pose when catastrophe strikes:

"What do we do now?"

Before I could answer with the obvious retort—"Bail!"—we were hit broadside by a huge gust of wind and knocked over, this time sideways into the water. And it's true what they say. Everything happened as though we were in slow motion. I literally felt like the Six Million Dollar Man as the boat seemingly took forever to capsize, all the time thinking to myself, "I can't believe this is happening to me!"

Of course, this had never happened to either of us before.

Immediately, we found ourselves treading water, separated from the boat. The sailboat, by now, had completely gone belly-up.

Seeing that we were both all right as we bobbed about in what felt increasingly like the Sacandaga Ocean, I directed Barbara to swim over to the boat. Meanwhile, I tried to scoop up all the loose items that had separated from the sailboat, and that were now quickly being dispersed in an ever widening pattern.

I was only partially successful. Davy Jones's locker ultimately claimed a pair of sneakers, a rain jacket, and my favorite sailing hat. Undoubtedly, some scuba diver will find these dubious treasures of the deep some day and wonder what kind of misadventure had befallen their owner.

Slowly, pushing the items I was able to gather in front of me, I was able to make my way over to the boat. It took only a few minutes to secure these items to the sailboat using what props we had at hand.

Strange as it may sound, during this whole time we were totally oblivious to the fact that about half a mile away on the shore, a huge number of people from the Sacandaga Trailer Park had gathered to watch and wonder what our fate would be.

Unaware of the entertainment we had become, and the free show we were providing, my only concern was in getting the boat upright again. The last thing I wanted was to be slowly swept towards Sand Island, which was another mile or so off to my right.

After some frustrating moments trying to communicate with each other, with waves and wind constantly drowning out the spoken word, Barbara and I finally got our act together. With some effort, we got the boat back over onto its side so that the sail was now floating just slightly under but parallel to the water's surface.

By now, Barbara had climbed up onto the keel.

"Think heavy!" I yelled up to Barbara. She, of course, winced at the thought.

While Barbara tried leveraging the keel using her weight, I pushed upward on the sail and mast at the same time, hoping to spill some of the water out of the sail and to see the boat suddenly bob upright like a cork.

Nothing happened.

Barbara came up with a better idea. We switched places. Now I was riding high on the keel and Barbara was pushing up on the mast.

"Think heavy!" Barbara yelled out encouragingly, obviously beginning to enjoy herself more.

And without any further ado the boat immediately popped upright, just as the textbooks had said it would.

"Hurrah!" we both yelled simultaneously. Things were looking better.

But the feeling of triumph was short-lived. The boat was full of water. In fact, it looked more like a bath tub. Where was the bailer? "Oh yes," I muttered to myself as I grabbed onto the upper half of a Clorox bottle. Although the Clorox bottle had worked fine for our canoe, it really didn't look equal to the task of bailing out the sailboat.

Making matters worse, the boat was riding very low in the water due to all of the extra weight, and water kept coming in as each new wave broke over us.

"The jib...the jib...." Barbara kept mumbling.

"What?" I yelled over the sound of crashing waves, thinking that maybe Barbara was becoming hypothermic and incoherent. We had been wet and exposed for some time now, and early fall was blowing its cool breeze.

"You shouldn't have raised the jib," Barbara yelled back.

Naturally, I had opinions of a contrary nature, and so we seized the opportunity to debate the matter for several minutes.

The people on shore, unfortunately, were deprived of the entertainment value of this private conversation.

Later, after feeling sufficiently heated up from the debate, we both agree to put our energies into getting us and the boat back to shore.

Meanwhile, however, fate had begun to smile on us. The distant hum of a motor jarred us into awareness that a rescue party was fast approaching—our neighbor, Bob.

Although I am not a fan of motorized craft, I was sure glad that day to see Bob and his power boat. Yet, even with his huge aluminum craft, Bob was being tossed about like a rag doll.

I also became aware that Barbara's son, Matthew, who occupied a small summer trailer by the lake, was swimming towards us and closing in fast. By one of those strange coincidences that always seems to happen, he and his fiancée had been out on the beach and had watched the whole incident unfold. Matthew had waded into the water, walking out several hundred yards before the water got above his chest. From there, the old crawl stroke took over.

Seeing now that we were going to be rescued, and slowly realizing his own increasing vulnerability (he was not wearing a wet suit or life jacket, and the water was cold) Matthew wisely headed back to shore. Undoubtedly, Matthew had provided an unexpected additional moment of drama for the onlookers lining the beach.

Bob threw me a line which I quickly connected to the bow of our sailboat. For several moments I continued bailing out water, but it felt like I was working against the lake with a thimble.

Barbara had already swum over to Bob's boat and was safely aboard. I now followed suit. Of course I had to macho it, pulling myself up and over into Bob's craft single-handedly. I didn't want anyone thinking that I was more of a wimp than I was already feeling.

In the roller coaster waves the trip back proved to be a very sporting journey, but uneventful.

Feeling both appreciative and needing some quick body heat, I gave Bob a big hug, and then jumped off the boat at shore.

Back at the camp, it only took about ten minutes to bail out the boat using the proper equipment, and everything seemed back to normal again, except my nerves.

As I now write this essay, the *Sac* is once again at full strength and capacity. I can hear its power as the waves unceasingly pound away at the shoreline, beckoning me back for another adventure.

This time we'll be readier!

BIBLIOGRAPHY

Aber, Ted, and Stella King. *The History of Hamilton County* (Great Wilderness Books, 1965).

Boos, John E. *The Sacandaga Valley* (Johnson Press).

Clarkson, Elisabeth Hudnut. *An Adirondack Archive: The Trail to Windover* (North Country Books, Inc., 1993).

Cross, David, and Joan Potter. *Adirondack Firsts* (Pinto Press, 1992).

Dunn, Violet B. (Editor-in-chief). *Saratoga County Heritage* (no publisher or date listed).

Gazda, Edward R. *Place Names in New York* (Gazda Associates, 1997).

Hart, Larry. *The Sacandaga Story: A Valley of Yesteryear* (Lary Hart, 1967).

Laing, Linda. *Guide to Adirondack Trails: Southern Region* (Adirondack Mountain Club, 1994).

McMartin, Barbara. *Discover the Adirondacks Series* (various publishers, including Backcountry, Lake View, New Hampshire, and Adirondack Mountain Club).

McMartin, Barbara. *50 Hikes in the Adirondacks* (Back Country Publications, 1988).

McMartin, Barbara. *Hides, Hemlocks, and Adirondack History* (North Country Books, Inc., 1992).

Morris, Nancy. *In Days Past* (Greenfield Press, 1995).

Proskin, Alec C. *Adirondack Canoe Waters: South and West Flow* (The Adirondack Mountain Club, 1986).

Roseberry, C. R. *From Niagara to Montauk* (State University of New York Press, Albany, 1982).

Sawyer, Donald J. *They Came to Sacandaga* (Prospect Books, 1976).

Shaw, Kenneth B. *Broadalbin: Then and Now* (The Franklin Press, 1973).

Shaw, Kenneth B. *Bleeker, Mayfield, Perth: A Pictorial History* (The Franklin Press, 1974).

Thomas, Lester St. John. *Timber, Tannery & Tourists* (Committee on Publication of Local History, 1979).

Author not listed. *The Illustrated History of Montgomery & Fulton Counties, New York* (Heart of the Lake Publishing, 1981 reprinted from an 1878 manuscript).